AUTUMN LEAVE

AUTUMN LEAVE

A Season in France

Michele Guinness

Authentic

MILTON KEYNES ● COLORADO SPRINGS ● HYDERABAD

15 14 13 12 11 10 09   8 7 6 5 4 3 2

Reprinted 2009
This edition published 2009 by Authentic Media
9 Holdom Avenue, Bletchley, Milton Keynes, MK1 1QR, UK
1820 Jet Stream Drive, Colorado Springs, CO 80921, USA
OM Authentic Media, Medchal Road, Jeedimetla Village,
Secunderabad 500 055, A.P., India
www.loveauthentic.com

Authentic Media is a division of Biblica UK, previously IBS-STL UK. Biblica
UK is limited by guarantee, with its registered office at Kingstown
Broadway, Carlisle, Cumbria, CA3 0HA. Registered in England & Wales No.
1216232. Registered charity in England & Wales No. 270162 and Scotland
No. SCO40064

British Library Cataloguing in Publication Data
A catalogue record for this book is available from the British Library

ISBN-13: 978-1-85078-832-4

Cover Design by Suzi Perkins
Print Management by Adare
Printed in Great Britain by J.F. Print, Sparkford

For all my wonderful new friends
in France

to all my wonderful new friends
in France

Contents

Grateful Acknowledgements to:

Bishop Nicholas and St Tees in Lancaster, for loving us enough to give us leave. Patrick and Marinette and all at the Église Evangelique de Montmorillon for their love and the warmth of their welcome. Ruth Hassall for checking the manuscript and making suggested improvements. Dave and Meriel Cumming for the endless decorating and varnishing. David and Wendy Lewis for teaching two remedial twitchers to know their birds, and for the garden benches to watch them. Pat and Stephen Travis, Chris and John Elliott for the wonderful gift of trees. Joel and Sarah for all their creativity, especially in having Livvy and Reuben to inspire our efforts. Abby, for enjoying it so much, and making the effort to improve her French. Ali Hull of Authentic for being such a challenging, stimulating editor. Peter, my wonderful trench digger and dam maker, without whose companionship and love, none of this would have been possible. And our Heavenly Estate Agent who provided us with an earthly tabernacle more wonderful than we ever imagined having.

May

We didn't intend to buy a house in France. Like a pair of kids ogling the goodies in a toy shop, knowing they haven't enough pocket money, we gazed longingly at the estate agents' property boards and told ourselves that we were only window shopping.

To be honest, the idea of living in France had been a long-cherished, apparently unobtainable dream. Peter and I had always shared a passion for all things French. He was raised bilingual in Geneva, son of an ex-army padre who was involved in post-war refugee work, and an English Canadian mother. His English can still be a little quaint at times, as in 'Wait a little moment.' Fortunately, I have the gift of interpretation.

My degree was in French. In fact, during my third year of university, which I spent as a school *assistante* in Paris, I became close friends with a young Frenchwoman, one of nine daughters of a gracious Pentecostal pastor, who had succeeded in acquiring a quarter of his congregation and a very small bank account. At one evening service, I was asked to translate for a visitor from England, a young man who told a remarkable story of how around half the sixth form of his boarding school had become Christians after he and a friend had found themselves praying through the entire night for every member of their class. He suddenly turned to me and said, 'You'll know the first bloke who responded because he's at university with you. He met us as we were going back for breakfast and told us he'd woken up early and decided to read John's Gospel, though he'd never done anything like that before. Peter Guinness?'

I had a vague recollection of a nice pair of eyes and an attractive smile and when I got back to university in Manchester, bounced up to him, introduced myself and said we had French contacts. The current was immediate – at least, I felt it, even if he claimed he didn't. So when my French friend married the other half of the all-night praying pair, Peter's closest school friend, and we both went to Paris for the wedding, I took him to Versailles for the day, convinced he would quickly submit to both its charms and mine. He didn't. It took four long years of supernatural patience on my part before the French connections were finally sealed.

In the early days of our marriage, we always thought they were more than a mere coincidence and anticipated that any day would herald the appearance of neon-light style arrows in the sky pointing us to the heathens across the Channel, especially when George Verwer of Operation Mobilisation announced that, after Turkey, France was the most spiritually desolate country in Europe. But it was a favourite British holiday hang-out, so never seen as a serious mission field. Which church would ever take a life of hot croissants, fresh baguettes, wonderful cheeses and good red wine as a genuine missionary calling? It just wasn't hair-shirt enough.

The illuminated guidance never came. Ordination to the Church of England did, but throughout twenty-five years and three churches, the sense of calling to our nearest European neighbours never really diminished.

So here we are, back in France after many years' absence, on holiday in La Rochelle for three weeks, with retirement on the horizon – and no roots anywhere. I have always found rootlessness one of the hardest parts of Christian ministry. Thirty years of other people's taste in tiles, kitchen tops and vinyl, of never seeing the bushes you plant bigger than your kneecaps and of knowing that, at the end of it all, wherever you are, you will have to leave it all behind and move on. As a cost, of course, it doesn't begin to compare with the daily trials and dangers facing Christians in the persecuted church, who stand to lose much more than their homes. At the turn of the twentieth century, my Jewish ancestors, forced to flee the pogroms of Eastern Europe, were familiar with that sense of displacement – until they settled in the UK, prospered and became comfortable in the land of their exile. In a sense, 'exile', not comfort, should be the Christian's normal state – the 'here we have no lasting city' unease with the bricks and mortar tents that eat up an entire income and will one day be subject to the whims of successive, unborn generations, who will rip out those ultramodern kitchens and bathrooms we thought were the ultimate necessity. Even so, I have worried about our retirement, about taking out a mortgage, making new friends and discovering a new community in our relative dotage.

Manifestly, it won't be here in France, I say to myself, as we study the house prices and sigh, loudly. There are plenty of barns, outhouses and run-down farmhouses to be had – with no foundations, no proper plumbing, no electricity, damp in the plaster, woodworm in the timbers and daylight visible through the roof. They are affordable. The repairs are probably not. We have heard so many horror stories over the years of people who pursued the French dream, bought a romantic, crumbling pile, then found it had swallowed up all their savings by the time they had a roof over their heads, running water and plaster on the walls.

We are distracted from our reveries for a day or two. Peter's older brother, who lives in the States and whom we rarely see, happens to be coming to La Rochelle for a couple of days to try out the latest, crew-less, one-man yachts. His appetite for adventure never seems to diminish and his wife now feels that sailing the Atlantic and the Med in his ripening years requires all the extra technology he can lay his hands on. My brother-in-law and his wife are great fun and we thoroughly enjoy the pleasure and pretence of purchasing a boat, taking great care not to give too much away about our own unpromising little quest. After all, every summer for years we have been taking advantage of his immense generosity in letting us use his lovely Ibiza home for our holidays. On the last night John tells us that he has given a loan to Peter's sister to enable her to buy a property in the USA. He would like to do the same for us. We can barely sleep for excitement. With his gift, our savings and a mortgage, there's an outside chance the French dream might actually materialise.

But where do we start? Paddy, who with her husband owns the lovely *gîte* we're staying in, sends us off to see Paula, an English estate agent who assists hordes of marauding English to acquire the French property of their fantasies. Paula is convinced she will find something to our taste at our price but after trawling through all the books, I'm not too sure. Her sales pitch is interrupted by a phone call – an Englishman who can't sell his home and agrees to reduce the price for a quick sale. Even from where we are, on the other side of the desk and phone, his impatience and stress is palpable. Not a good sign.

'He shouldn't have put in those en suite bathrooms – a big mistake,' Paula confides. 'Head for bed and you fall into the toilet.'

Three days later we do the Paula tour – six houses in as many hours. I end up feeling like someone who has had too many cream cakes – sickly but dissatisfied. None are just right. There were 1950s houses with paper stuffed in the skirting boards to keep out the cold; traditional French farmhouses known as *longères*, where the rooms are laid out in a row and you have to walk through every other room in the house to get to your bedroom; cottages facing east-west as most French houses do, their only view their neighbours' garden furniture; barely-modernised cottages attached to vast, neglected sheds just waiting for someone to 'see their potential', according to their sellers, who manifestly didn't, or hadn't the energy or finances if they did. We even visited an antique car enthusiast whose six oak barns provided immaculate sleeping space for his unique, exquisitely restored collection of Fords, while his own bedroom was the size of the monkey's cage at the zoo.

'I don't sleep with ze wife,' he offered by word of explanation, with a wink. 'I send her to work in Bordeaux. Me, I prefer to sleep with ze cars.'

'Now this property could be a bargain,' whispered Peter, fondling the fat oak beams. 'Each of these barns would make a fabulous *gîte*. Am I called to give up the ministry for the letting business?' he wonders, with a certain wistfulness.

At home in England, our friendly builder who comes to repair the vicarage from time to time cannot conceive of how my engineer of a husband could have jilted his love of carpentry, plumbing and wiring for the lot of a clergyman. 'It's a daft job Peter does,' he tells me repeatedly, 'and what's more, there's no money in it. Tell you what, tell him to be ready with his lunch box Monday morning at 8 am sharp and I'll pick him up. Business is brisk. I could do with a mate.'

On difficult days it's been tempting. As is the idea at this moment of building several modern *gîtes* out of beautiful, ancient oak beams. Peter remembers his calling with a sigh and taps them an affectionate, if reluctant, farewell.

Neither of us enjoy spending a very great deal of money. It's not all it's cracked up to be. In fact, spending virtually all one's savings on a large materialistic purchase can seriously disturb the spiritual equilibrium. I see-saw from one perspective to another in my effort to handle it. On the one hand, with millions starving in the world, how can I have the gall to pray for a French house – even if it is our one and only home? Maybe we should stop looking, abandon the idea altogether – unless one happens to be dropped onto our path from the heavenly estate agent, who has every property on earth on his books. On the other hand, my Jewish Mama has always believed in the concept of *bescherret* or 'meant to be.' How much more should I, with the additional benefit of Christian faith, trust that if we are meant to be in France, there is a 'meant to be' house somewhere, just for us?

In the end we give ourselves to the end of the second week of our holiday. If nothing seems right, we'll abandon the manic newspaper scouring and endless discussion, lay down the dream and simply enjoy our last week. Otherwise, we'll go home exhausted.

June

Only a few days to go before our last week. Even on holiday I like to spend the first waking moments in reflection, meditation and prayer – even if the mind has a mind of its own and goes on a wander. What I do absorb sets the tone for the day. It's never quite the same if I put it off until later. More often than not, later never comes.

I'm reading though the Old Testament and, looking out over the acid green, duck-weedy waterways of La Venise Verte, open the book of Joshua. The Hebrew warrior Caleb promises the hand of his daughter, Achsah, to whoever takes the city of Kiriath-sepher. A bit free with his daughter's future, isn't he? Might this be one way of attracting a new assistant minister to our church? Whoever is brave enough to take on the job can have our daughter as a bonus – presuming it is a man, of course. No, our daughter definitely wouldn't like it.

But Achsah, the clever cookie, is no pushover either. Water is essential to make the desert blossom, so she touches her father for a far better dowry – upper and lower springs to water the field he has given her.

I call to Peter in the sitting room and tell him that my reading seems significant somehow. 'There's something about these upper and lower springs. We both like looking at water. Should we be looking for somewhere with water?'

He doesn't dismiss me, which is disturbing. Not so much as a chortle. All he says is, 'Not another pre-requisite.'

'Okay,' I shout. 'Ignore me.'

Paddy is out early working in the garden. Letting property looks like hard work. All the same, it's work I wouldn't mind being blessed with. 'If you give us a property, God,' I whisper, 'we'll share it with our cash-strapped friends in full-time ministry.' There's nothing like trying to twist God's arm.

Later, I go out to tell Paddy that we seem to have exhausted Paula's supply of houses and nothing she has shown us seems right. 'We saw some rum places before we found this one,' she laughs. 'One of them was owned by a sweet little old pair, who showed us into an upstairs room that had nothing in it except a wardrobe. Inside the wardrobe were steps leading up into an attic. I thought, I'm off to Narnia – until we got to the top. All the walls were covered in black velvet. The ceiling was all mirrors and the only furniture in the room was a double bed on the floor. Our faces must have been a picture. The old man winked at us and the woman grinned. Evidently this room was their pride and joy. We managed a smile of appreciation. When you're house-hunting you have to be so careful not to hurt anyone's feelings. The French, eh? Age doesn't dampen their ardour.'

Apparently there are one thousand estate agents in La Rochelle. How would we ever get round them all? Their share is 10% of the sale – a reasonable amount in the days when houses cost a mere £14,000 – but not now the English have devoted themselves to a serious inflation of the market. When will the French wake up and refuse to pay it?

Meanwhile, Peter has been studying a property guide he picked up at La Rochelle airport when we arrived in the country ten days ago. I peek over his shoulder. He has ringed a house that looks idyllic. It has its own little lake.

'That looks lovely,' I enthuse.

'Hardly Lake Geneva,' he replies wistfully, as child-hood memories of their rented flat overlooking the lake come flooding back. 'It's little more than a pond.'

'And we're not exactly the Rothschilds,' I remind him. 'Anyway, it'll be gone.' I'm a martyr to disbelief. 'Or else there's a catch, at that price, but ring the agent all the same.'

A quarter of an hour later he rushes into the garden to find me. 'It hasn't gone,' he says excitedly, 'but the house is a long way inland, so be prepared for a trek. We're going on Friday, D-Day, our last day!'

On Friday morning I start the next book in the Old Testament – Judges. I wasn't looking forward to the bloodthirsty bits – not the cheeriest way to start the day, especially pre-breakfast. But in chapter 1, to my amazement, the story of Achsah is repeated verbatim. Why had I never noticed that before? And why was it there?'

'I've got it again,' I call to Peter.

'You've got what? A cold? A headache? An itch?'

'There's definitely something in these springs. Achsah's – not the bed's.'

The first moment we set eyes on it, we realise the house isn't at all what we envisaged – old, rambling and charming, waiting for a little, manageable, loving renovation. It's modern, square and compact. On the other hand, old means damp-ridden, freezing and impractical, while new is insulated, double-glazed and cosy. It might not be romantic but it is cheap to run and ready to live in. It faces south and the sun streams in – unusual in France, where the natives prefer the cool and keep it out but a must for Peter, who loves light and is thinking free heat in the winter. Not only that but a large verandah with a pleasant if not stunning outlook, over a man-made pond, has been glassed in, its windows acting as virtual solar panels. With the property comes two large fields, should the urge to banish the grandchildren or run a camp-site ever take us.

The practicalities of the property appear to support signs of even greater significance. On the narrow country road leading up to the gate we cross a little stream called the Asse. Not quite Achsah – but near enough to make me sit up. As we turn into the driveway, our former used-car dealer estate agent points at the large field on the far side of the house, which is covered in bales of hay.

'Henri, the owner has just mown the field,' he says. 'You see those two green patches at the top and bottom of the lake? One is the upper spring that feeds into it. The other is the lower spring, that flows from it into the Asse.'

After that, I think we know we are simply exploring the extraordinary gift that has indeed fallen at our feet.

In many ways I can't quite take it in and a sudden wave of panic engulfs me at the thought of actually committing our entire life's savings. I begin to think of reasons why the whole idea is a big mistake.

'It is a long way out into the country, very cut off,' I say to the estate agent. After all, though we aren't exactly Darby and Joan yet, this is our retirement we're planning. How long will we remain mobile? I'm given to bouts of depressing realism.

'This is France,' he laughs. 'Don't think distance. There's a huge hypermarket in the nearest big town only twenty minutes away. You'll barely pass a car there and back.'

I am still struggling with the magnitude of the commitment two days later when we go back to meet Henri Bouvier, the young farmer who owns the property and the land around it. He's a good-looking, clean-shaven man, with a strong, local accent that makes his French almost unintelligible to two politely-spoken foreigners. We nod enthusiastically, the way people do when they don't really understand what's being said to them, each aware that our other half is piecing snippets together, in the hope that between us we may have the gist of the conversation.

'He's selling up, he says, because he's too far away from the centre of his farm – it takes him twenty minutes by tractor,' I whisper to Peter the moment Henri moves out of earshot.

We find it hard to understand why Henri would want to abandon a house he so lovingly built only seven years ago and that manifestly still has a special place in his heart. The dashing bachelor brought his bride here and they have a little girl, Chantal.

'Are the English welcome in the area?' I ask. The rustic dialect has made me realise we are well and truly out in the sticks. 'After all, it must feel like a bit of an invasion.'

'You'll be the first and only English in our hamlet. We don't mind you coming here if you speak our language and learn our ways. We just don't understand why you English leave England, then try and recreate it here.'

No holding back then. At least he's honest.

We definitely don't want to do that, we tell him but it feels rather feeble when the truth is that the house could well be empty most of the year for several years and that will hardly contribute to the locals' sense of community.

'What about that little wood opposite, on the other side of the lake?' Peter pushes him. We are worried about it being sold off and the land developed. 'Can we buy it? Could you approach the family who owns it and ask them for us?'

Is it my imagination or is his response just a little too hasty?

'Ah, non, non, non, I can't do that.' Then, as if by way of explanation, he says in a more conciliatory manner,

'If I let them know you want it, they will double the price.'

As we take our leave, I tell Henri we're thrilled with the house. It feels like a happy house, I say, enthusiastically. Henri simply looks at me and says nothing. Or is that just my imagination?

We lunch at the dingy, rather basic hotel in the centre of the nearby village, joining a crowd of local workers in caps and braces with expanding girths and diminishing teeth. 'What's the *menu du jour*?', asks our estate agent. He speaks virtual French fluently. It just sounds like English. The waitress shrugs, unsmiling. Pot luck, he sniffs. Stuffed tomatoes are followed by a ratatouille and a bean salad, *roti de boeuf* and chips, cheese, dessert, a flagon of wine, a bottle of water, freshly ground coffee and all the bread you can eat for a few euros. I'll opt for the pot luck menu any day.

On our way back to La Rochelle, we pop into the French estate agents selling the property, to tie up some of the administrative details.

'How do you discover any problems regarding your property?' we ask the French agent.'Is there such a thing as a search?' No one had shared that crucial piece of information. He shakes his head and suggests we visit the Mayor. The Mayor always knows everything – every local and historic argument. But we have no time left that day.

'Never mind. What can go wrong?' I ask Peter, as we walk out of the door.

Travelling back through our nearest 'big' town – the one with the hypermarket and huge population of around five thousand – we see a banner stretched from one lamp-post to another, welcoming visitors to 'Montmorillon, City of the Book, Home to Writers and Calligraphers.'

It seems apt somehow.

The following morning a thought occurs to me. 'Okay then, Mr Walking Concordance,' I call from the bedroom to the sitting-room, as I look at the story of Achsah again. 'Tell me what Kiriath-sepher means – the name of the land Caleb gives his daughter as her inheritance.' I should know but my ancient Hebrew is a bit rudimentary. As a child I learnt to read it fluently and still can but translating it was another matter. The important thing in the synagogue was to look as if you could follow the service – even if you didn't understand a word. *Sepher,* I suddenly remember, is 'book' as in *Sepher Torah* – the book of the law. But Kiriath?

There's a lengthy silence from the other room as the computer slowly and painfully loads firewalls, virus protectors and finally the large biblical concordance programme. Oh bring back paper, it's so much quicker. And then there's a roar of laughter.

'You'll never guess,' Peter guffaws.

He brings me a mug of coffee, puts it down on my bedside table and kisses me. 'Kiriath is city. Kiriath-sepher is City of the Book. Couldn't really be clearer, could it?'

'X marks the spot. The end of the adventure.'

'Oh no,' replies Peter. 'I have a feeling this is just the beginning.'

We just happen to have a three month sabbatical booked for September and no plans – except to explore retirement possibilities.

'I think we're meant to come back to France for our sabbatical, that is, if we can buy the house in time.'

September

It seems very strange to be driving out of Lancaster on a Sunday morning, rather than in, with many of our congregation going in the opposite direction on their way to church. They, of course, are totally unaware that behind the wheel of the large hired van staggering past them to the M6, stacked with surplus vicarage furniture, bargain BHS sale bedding and Wilkinson's kitchen knick-knacks, is their vicar setting off on his sabbatical.

We never intended spending our sabbatical in France. Most of our colleagues have followed more worthy pursuits – long silent retreats, visits to expanding churches to learn their methodology, intensive theological study, educational and instructive trips to poverty- and AIDS-beleaguered areas to see the needs first-hand. And we are going to France to set up home. Have altruism and the need for self-improvement deserted us completely? This seems terribly dull, unadventurous and unspiritual by comparison. Yet it seems to make sense.

The sale of the house was completed in a record three months, presenting us with a God-given opportunity not only to escape the telephone and diary for an extended period but to see if it is realistic to retire over the Channel. The idea might seem idyllic but in reality the culture is very different and church life is in many places virtually non-existent. I contacted the Intercontinental Church Society chaplain for the area before we left and discovered that his parish in our part of Western France, is the size of Wales. I know enough about ex-pats to realise that Anglican worship abroad has to reflect a wide variety of traditions. There will always be some who wanted a slice of nostalgia – even if church has never been one of their priorities before. We could be travelling well over an hour on Sundays for that quintessential slice of good old, little England – the Book of Common Prayer. I'm glad some people develop a sudden attachment to it, in an environment that might help them find faith. My Jewish background means that I have none. We will be looking for a French-speaking congregation – if one is to be found.

I must say that my pathological distaste for tales of God's direct intervention in great materialistic purchases hasn't altered – especially after two weeks' speaking at conferences in South Africa just before we set off. We visited the Alexandra township where folk live in makeshift dwellings of cardboard, tin and corrugated iron and I felt more than just a little overwhelmed and ashamed at the luxury of our possessions. On the other hand, it would be churlish not to see the French house at the very least as a gift.

En route to the Channel crossing we stop to join traditional English Sunday worship. The faithful are flocking into Ikea in their hordes, carried along on a tidal wave of adoration. We allow ourselves fifteen minutes to pick up two swivel chairs and several packet of serviettes, (my husband knows his priorities) and it becomes obvious that the worshipful masses, standing silently before mouthwatering displays of Molechbo, Dagonviks and Baaltorps, resent having two loose cannons disrupt their slow, reverent passage through the temple. 'Bloody hell', shouts one woman angrily, as we say a brief, 'Excuse me', and shoot past. Clearly, we aren't following the correct order of service, or treating the occasion with the due seriousness and dignity it deserves. It is salutary to see the number of cars packing the car park. Church-goers never have the opportunity to suss out the opposition. Surely there are better ways of spending a weekend than assembling a flat-pack wardrobe? But the church isn't an attractive enough alternative.

We spend the night in Calais – Europe's largest grave-yard. I'm revamping my inner images of a country where the locals sit up all night in brasseries and berets, drinking red wine and saying, '*Hein*' and 'Ooh la la.' Nine at night and not a soul in the streets, not a light in a house, no food to be had. The hotel is cheap – and not very cheerful, the mattresses made of concrete, the tap dripping incessantly. At 2 am I finally succumb to taking a sleeping pill – but even that doesn't help.

Monday, 18th September

We set off from Calais at speed, as we have an appointment that afternoon to insure our new home. Useless with directions at the best of times, I'm of no use to Peter at all today. The sleeping pill has finally kicked in. It takes me all my time to open my eyes and be civilised when I do.

Thankfully, we reach Montmorillon on time. Our insurance broker, Olivier Auneau, is one of those handsome Frenchmen who knows he is drop dead gorgeous. He's perky and a joker to boot. 'My name is Monsieur "Oh no" – oh no, funny, get it, eh?' He slaps his hand on the table and laughs uproariously. 'Especially when you consider we have to insure against falling trees, floods, fire and all the things that make the Englishman shout "Oh no!" and have to call me.'

His PA has manifestly heard this routine many times and barely manages a smile. We are more polite and indulge him with a forced guffaw or two.

'But oh, these English, they are innocents abroad – like little lambs.'

In time to come I will wonder whether Monsieur Auneau has the gift of prophecy.

We spend the night *chez* our English estate agent, as he runs a B and B alongside his many other talents. Yet another dripping tap. I am pursued by them. It's like one of my worst speaking engagement trips. Hosts are immensely hospitable but, like most of us, inured to the sounds in their own homes – the creaky floorboards, rumble of traffic and the ticking, or worse, chiming clock. Guests are not. The effects of last night's sleeping tablet have well and truly worn off.

Tuesday, 19th September

Today the house becomes ours in a formal transfer ceremony reminiscent of a registry office wedding. The vendor, buyer and their spouses sit side by side with their solicitors and estate agents in waiting, while *Maitre Notaire* makes her humorous best of the ninety minute, legal process. 'Do you, Monsieur et Madame Guinness, take this house in full agreement with all the rules and regulations of the government, the commune, the legal system, the banks . . .'

We are asked to assent to the fact that this was a second home. 'But our one and only,' I pipe up. 'The one we live in is not our own.'

'Ah, *un presbytère*,' they all concede. Indulgent smiles all round – an emotional moment. As *Maitre Notaire* declares the formalities over and wishes us '*Felicitations*' and joy in our new home, I fully expect her to encourage the two happy couples to kiss each other. It seems a great omission not to be able to pull a bottle of Bollinger out of my bag.

Then we and our entourage repair to our new property, where the previous owners, Henri and Madeleine, make an almost tearful handover of the keys, show us how to work the central heating and explain which plants needed protection in the winter.

'This is very hard,' says Madeleine, an attractive young French woman, who manages to make a pair of denims look the latest in chic. 'Henri and I built this house together. We love it.'

'How could you leave it?' I ask her, puzzled. We have established a rapport fairly quickly.

'Ah,' she sighs mysteriously, 'Perhaps I'll explain one day.'

Finally, everyone leaves and we are completely alone – for three months. Writing a biography of the Guinness family some years ago, I discovered that one of the trials faced by pioneer missionary couples was being thrown upon each other for all emotional and conversational needs. It can put the strongest relationships under pressure. How will ours stand up to the strain?

For a while we wander around in a daze, opening and reopening cupboard doors, experimenting with switches, reading meters and flushing the loos. Am I glad that we abandoned any idea of doing up a wreck or an old barn. At least our seven-year old house is habitable. But as we empty the van and our 'mass' of belongings are swallowed up and become a tiny pile in the middle of one room, the enormity of what we have done hits us like a bolt from a crossbow. This isn't a dress that's a big mistake, or even a car that turns out to be a disaster. This is nearly thirty years of savings. Besides, the financial cost has just begun. We've only a fridge, a basic two-ring cooker donated by thoughtful church members after clearing a deceased parent's house and a mound of theological books for study purposes. The latter make very decent bedside tables, alongside the futon mattresses we lay out on the bedroom floor – Peter being too weary to construct the bases with their endless slats. In the dark we join hands and give our new home back to God. It's the only safe place for it. We know no one and suddenly this seems very late in life to be setting out on a grand adventure.

But no dripping taps – hallelujah.

Wednesday, 20th September

Peter has been awake for hours when I finally come to and he's studying the deeds.

'Look,' he says with excitement. 'The house was never designed to face south. It was meant to face east-west like most French houses but the land was too rocky and the foundations had to be altered and the building moved. Perfect for us. Isn't that wonderful?'

We set off to the hypermarket for a mega shop. It's fun surveying and sniffing the French delicacies – the rows of extraordinary, polka dot sausages hanging in the *charcuterie* section, the luscious-looking, oozing cheeses, the wealth of fresh, crispy bread in every shape and size. I want to try them all but Peter is chivvying me on – he hates food shopping and there are beds to be bought. All is well until we pop into the electrical section and try to buy a washing machine. Our cash card is rejected. We ring the Post Office in some dismay. We had opened an account with their banking facility when we were in France in June.

'Ah, Madame,' they say genially, 'You have only just used up your credit limit for this week.'

I am almost winded with the shock.

'Three hundred euros a week, less than two hundred pounds? But we haven't started yet. We have to buy an oven, beds, furniture, a washing machine, tumble drier, garden mower...'

'I'm afraid three hundred euros is your limit,' says the Post Office, curtailing me in full flow.

'But it's our money. We put lots of it into the account – as much as we could find.'

Watching my distress with some evident fascination, the sales assistant suddenly asks in a stage whisper, 'Have you a cheque book?'

He is evidently used to this. We nod dumbly.

'I take cheques,' he says, at exactly the same moment as the voice on the other end of the phone says, 'Do you have your cheque book?'

'Cheques,' Peter grumbles, as he writes one out, 'Paper money. It's archaic.'

We only have our van for a fortnight, before the church administrator comes out in our car and takes it home, as we can't afford any more insurance. So we have to buy all the big stuff as quickly as possible. We drive fifty miles into Limoges, our nearest city and look for anything vaguely resembling a furniture shop. None appear to have any beds in stock – not of the quality our hyper-active, bed-expert son, Joel, has told us we have to have, at any rate. We have promised we won't skimp on this vital purchase. Eventually, in what appears to be an equivalent of MFI, we ask them what they do have in stock and they reassure us, with the appropriate snoring noises, that our guests will pass the night in '*le comfort maximum.*' We tell them we'll make up our minds by the end of the day. We are still, at this stage, into comparing prices.

By now it's midday and all the shops have shut – until 2pm. The cafés and bars are full of people relaxing, chatting, laughing and enjoying the autumn sunshine as they down six courses and half a litre of red wine.

'How do they ever do any work in the afternoon?' I ask Peter. 'On the other hand, perhaps we English would all be more productive if we had a decent break in the middle of the day. Maybe the French have it right after all.'

Still, it's frustrating for those of us who aren't used to it, so we decide to head for the town centre, where, apparently, the shopping malls do stay open at lunchtime.

Parking takes forever, because we don't have the proper tokens for the meter and don't know where to find them. That established, we finally stumble across Darty, an impressive electrical shop that appears to have all we need, not knowing that Darty is in fact the proud new owner of Comet. The service is exemplary. Nothing is too much trouble.

'Ah, now you would like a kettle, Madame. I only do ovens. Can I hand you over to my colleague who is a specialist in the small electrical items department?'

It's Britain in the 1960s, *à la* 'Are You Being Served' – quaint but pleasant. We receive undivided attention for well over an hour. Or perhaps the sales people, on commission, are used to the English making bulk purchases. I have never bought so many goods all at once. It should be fun. It isn't. I'm bored by machines and just want one that will do the job, whilst my mechanical engineer husband spends ages pouring over their various advantages and inadequacies. Also, shopping on this scale makes me giddy. I don't enjoy making big purchases in the UK where I know how to find what I want. Here, where populations are so much smaller, there is much less variety and choice and everything seems so expensive.

We order an oven, tumble drier and dishwasher. They will be delivered to our door in three days – just in time for the arrival of Joel and his wife Sarah, thank heavens. And no delivery charge. This is a miracle.

'But we live in the middle of the countryside,' Peter says, 'miles from anywhere.'

'Ah, Monsieur, we're used to that,' they smile, 'Everyone does.'

'At least we will be able to feed the family,' I sigh with relief. Jewish Mama to the last.

During Peter's lengthy and detailed discussions on the merits of plastic versus metal interior drums, I have been desperately ringing France Telecom on a mobile that seems to have minimal range, in an attempt to set up a land-line. There is no signal at all at our house, so it is imperative we have some means of contacting the outside world. Not only that – I need to have access to email to send the copy I have promised to my editor in England. Living out in the country as we do, we suspect that broadband is a non-starter and old-fashioned dial-up our only option. The problem is I don't know any of these words in French. I tried saying 'broadband' in my best French accent in one of the phone shops but only succeeded in making the sales assistant back away quickly with a frightened expression.

Despite my reasonable French, I struggle to understand what the operator at France Telecom is telling me. Then, just as she begins to make sense, the mobile cuts out. This happens several times. Finally, after around an eight minute conversation, just as the transaction is nearing completion, I lose her again. I'm beside myself and, to my ignominy, burst into tears in the middle of the shopping mall. 'This is all so stressful,' I sob, as Peter emerges from Darty flushed with his recent success, only to find a blubbering heap waiting for him. 'Time's running out. We'll never get back for the beds before the shop closes. We'll never find the shop again. I just can't do all this.'

A hug, a 'There, there' and a 'We've got a washing machine' work wonders, so I mop up and we set off and after half a dozen or so false starts, erroneous turns and terse recriminations, eventually find our shop shortly before the deadline for the pick-up point.

Wonder of wonders, in the middle of the beds department I have a clear signal and finally get through to France Telecom. There doesn't appear to be a piece of data they don't need. I empty the contents of my handbag on the floor – passport, driving licence, birth certificate, marriage certificate. The only thing they don't need is the record of my GCSEs. I don't understand which documents I'm supposed to have and the operator has to spell out the words patiently, letter by painful letter.

'Calm, chill,' I keep saying to myself. 'Don't have a nervous breakdown yet. Oh God, give me the vocabulary!'

I don't understand some of the code numbers she's after and throw my papers and documents in the air in desperation. Several of the shop staff rush to my aid, pointing to the relevant numbers in my passport and cheque book. This has become a communal activity. Finally, the operator tells me to take down an address in Bordeaux. Once I send in photocopies of all the appropriate paperwork I can have a land-line. I and everyone around me, cheer. Then she says it will take around three weeks.

'Three weeks!' I explode. 'Three weeks? We need it yesterday.'

The shop staff are bemused. 'This is France,' they laugh, pretending to hold a gun to their heads.

'If you deliver it all by hand – to our shop in Limoges – it will be quicker, Madame, maybe a few days.'

I look at my watch. My heart sinks. There is no way we can get back into town before closing time. It means we will have to make the hour-long journey back to Limoges as soon as we can. To my surprise, I then hear her say with real warmth in her voice, 'Well done, Madame, your French is excellent.'

'No it isn't,' I say miserably. 'I didn't get a lot of what you were saying.'

'Ah, that was heaven compared to what I normally deal with. Most English are impossible – no French at all.'

I thank her, wondering how they cope and hang up, feeling somewhat cheered.

We come away with five bed bases and six mattresses that will do nicely, cheaper than we intended. Only one bed base is on order. I will sleep tonight in my very own bed in my own home. Never has such a little thing seemed so very precious. I spare a prayer for all who are in prison for their faith, never knowing if they will lay their head on their own soft pillow ever again.

Friday, 22nd September

We are lost in Limoges – again – this time looking for furniture. We spent much of yesterday exploring the *brocantes* in our area – second-hand shops full of the most awful rubbish, decrepit, worm-ridden and falling apart. The French love heavy, dark furniture. It smells of disuse, moth balls and damp and isn't particularly cheap.

The local 'Eco Depot', purveyor of finished lines, was equally full of tat. There don't appear to be any bargains to be had, so we'll just have to trust the bank account is as elastic as it needs to be. If ever we find a furniture shop.

'Where are we?' Peter demands as he drives, leaning across me to read the large map on my lap, that all but covers the windscreen, passenger window, gear box and me. I manoeuvre it upside down – but that doesn't help. I can't see it anyway because I can't find my glasses and even if I could, it won't get me anywhere as I have the directional sense of a hamster. And, being France, there are no signs anyway.

'Why do you need a map?' I ask in exasperation, convinced he'll kill us both if he doesn't look at the road, rather than the map. 'You usually follow the sun.'

'I'm an "S," he snaps. 'I need to see where I'm going.'

We have both done the Myers Briggs personality analysis test. The huge differences between us are thrown into sharp, unforgiving relief in situations like these. In Myers Briggs terms, he is an introvert who does his machinations in his head. The 'S' means he needs to have the facts written out in front of him, the 'T' means he weighs them all up in a careful, orderly manner – and the 'P' means his deliberations are a waste of time since he postpones any final decision to the last possible moment because he's not too keen on tying up loose ends. I am the direct opposite. I do my thinking out loud, never read instructions, hate to let shopkeepers down and like to come away with all the ends tied up. The battle lines are drawn. And nowhere is that more apparent than in our attempts to get from A to B. A few months ago, a woman was found murdered on the hard shoulder of the M6 near where we live. I thought, 'Another poor soul who can't read maps.' Peter has an instinctive sense of direction but will he follow his instinct?

'The secret of using Myers Briggs,' I explain 'is to put your "shadow" side into practice – the bit you don't naturally use, so that you become more well-rounded. In this case the intuitive bit of you, Mr Intrepid Explorer. Or we can stop and ask for directions?'

Now that was a silly idea to suggest to a man. He stops the van with a crash of the gears, gathers the map together, studies it at length, mutters something about there being no junction numbers and starts the engine up again in silence.

'Well? Where are we going?' I ask tartly.

'Where's the sun?'

I know now what the Guinness missionary wives in Africa and China had to contend with.

Finally – with around half an hour to spare before the midday down-tools – we fall upon Atlas, the furniture shop recommended to us by the helpful staff in Darty. Our guide shakes our hand and introduces himself as Mr Payeratout – 'Mr Pay-for-it-all' – which seems an appropriate name for a salesman. Since he maintains a straight face at this revelation, so do we. But it's a struggle. At least he doesn't give the impression of a resentful tolerance of our Englishness.

I am beginning to have a glimpse into what it feels like to be an immigrant. We are part of a mighty force of Brits that has poured across the Channel in search of sunshine and cheap housing – economic migration in its most sophisticated disguise. We have bumped into our compatriots in every shop – usually buying the same goods – and often act as their interpreters. Despite the economic boost this influx undoubtedly brings the French, there is no doubt it can be a tad overwhelming, if not downright threatening, to have your familiar territory encroached upon by a mass of foreigners who only manage a pigeon version of your language and expect you to speak theirs. There is no overt hostility and most of the French seem welcoming but just occasionally I detect a certain *froideur* in the body language, an unspoken, 'I don't mind you being here but you're not really our sort', just enough to make me feel uncomfortable and apologetic. It's a strangely humiliating, isolating sort of feeling. Is this, I wonder, how we treat the Eastern Europeans who come to the UK looking for a better life and do the jobs that none of us ever want to do?

Yesterday I did try a 'This English invasion is our revenge for 1066' joke on one of the *brocanteurs* but the humour appeared to be lost in explanation.

When Peter rang France Telecom again this morning before we left, the operator put him on hold, forgot to turn off her loud speaker, then called to a colleague, 'Another of the English – but at least this one speaks French.' He was tempted to say, 'There's nothing wrong with his hearing either' but thought better of it.

We had a long conversation about immigration with Mr Pay-for-it-all. When Peter said he was a *pasteur*, the salesman asked him whether he had been closely following the criticisms of the Pope over his comments on the way Islam was taking over Europe and what he thought of it all. Because we don't have a television and haven't been listening to the radio, we haven't heard the news. I realise how out of touch we are. Part of me feels it's irresponsible not to be able to converse on current affairs, the other part thinks that not being bombarded with the world's pain may be the ultimate relief a sabbatical can give. We won't buy a television just yet.

'Is there much racism in your country?' asks M Payeratout. He had heard that there was, that relations with the Muslim community could be uneasy. Personally, he can't understand it. He has transferred his daughter to a primary school with a predominantly Muslim Arab intake, as they were so much nicer than the French – intelligent and charming, with a far greater appreciation of the gift of education. He feels Muslims are far better integrated in his country than they are in ours. He could be right and we are far too polite to mention recent race riots, or the resentment of laws that forbid any religious expression in schools.

There is no doubt that in France the Muslims have better PR than the Christians. We have seen a substantial number of white women wearing the hijab but not yet managed to locate a Protestant church service of any kind. None are advertised anywhere. When we eventually stumbled on an *église évangelique* in a high street on the way into Limoges, a sad-looking, out-of-date noticeboard told us services had been suspended during August. There was no information about what was happening in September and, since the church was a good hour from home, we weren't going to bother finding out.

While our salesman is holding forth on the shortcomings of the French educational system, Peter is writing down the price of every piece of furniture we think may be a possibility. To what end? I have all the figures in my head. Back in the car, while the shop is closed for lunch, he does copious calculations.

He wants the oak. I want pine.

'Whatever we get, it's going to break the bank,' he says.

It's not only driving in a strange place that puts stress on our relationship. I take great care in designing a room. I see it in my mind. I know the effect I want to achieve – modern farmhouse in this case. I know what will and what won't go, down to the last knick knack. To me, Peter is totally utilitarian. Any taste he has is subsumed to his need for comfort. This, combined with a colour sense that is akin to tone deafness in singing, is an affront to my wonderful aesthetic taste. He will, for example, sit on a puce-coloured armchair and seriously suggest we buy it, if it fits his torso and allows him to stretch out the legs that come with his six foot four frame. How could he even contemplate such a hideous item? Is he winding me up deliberately? His face is the very picture of innocence. He can't be but it still feels like time-wasting.

Fortunately the oak is unaffordable. The pine isn't! At 2pm on the dot I frog march him back into Atlas and say to the salesman, 'We'll have this, this, that and this – oh and that and yes, that too.'

We buy a dining-room table, eight chairs, a dresser for the china, bedside tables, chests of drawers, a wardrobe, a coffee table – the list seems endless and Peter is turning pale. But miracle of miracles – some of the items are three for the price of two. And then there is Monsieur Payeratout's discount. And, it appears, some of Peter's calculations in the van were seriously awry. The whole lot comes to at least a third less than we expected – a gift from heaven. Not only that but this is not Ikea. Everything is in stock except the wardrobe and we load it all into the van.

And there is still enough time to pay a visit to France Telecom. It's always hard to adapt to another culture. Anyone who decides to live in France has to learn to live with French bureaucracy – or spontaneously combust with frustration. There are rules for everything and since no one ever obeys them, they make some more. The European Community is awash with French-initiated legislation that no one but the English obeys. Travelling anywhere by car? You'll even need to carry a spare pair of glasses, if you wear them, or you may incur a large, instant fine.

We finally locate the shop down a back street in the centre of Limoges but it is ten minutes to the midday watershed and too late, says the assistant, with a dismissive wave, to do the necessary paperwork. 'Come back at 2pm.'

We concur without a murmur, having made up our minds to enjoy the compulsory two-hour lunch break like everyone else. We're on sabbatical. Our former, stressful lifestyle is not the best way to live. We're learning.

When, at 2.10pm, we finally wave our copious and detailed paperwork beneath the eyes of the sales representative, she barely looks at it and says lethargically, 'I'll switch you on.' So much for a three-week wait. Having a land-line turns out to be as easy as that – one press of a computer key and it's done. But we rejoice too soon.

'So now we can get online?' we ask with excitement.

She doesn't look up.

'*Non*, Madame. You'll have to ring the dedicated France Telecom number for that.'

'And how long will it take?' we dare to ask.

She shrugs.

Buying a mound of fascinating basics at Leclerc – light bulbs, plugs, wire, bathmat, clothes' rack, washing-up bowl and dish mop, works up an appetite. It's late and we don't know where to find a restaurant on this large trading estate. 'We'll eat here,' suggests Peter. I know better than to argue with a hungry man. It turns out to be Asda in school dinner mode. Of all the places that serve gourmet food in this land of excellence in haute cuisine, he brings me here. I look at him pulling faces as his fork reaches his mouth and try not to laugh. Ah well, I still love this man after all.

Saturday, 23rd September

Joel and Sarah arrive later today. I do so hope they will love this place, as Joel has loved his Uncle John's house in Ibiza, though I fear he might not. The Ibiza house once belonged to his grandparents who retired there and it was the only lasting and familiar home in a childhood that included five moves because of his father's ministry. No wonder he loved it. It was a taste of heaven. As soon as I arrived and smelled the pines, saw the vast expanse of sea below us, felt the soporific heat and heard the chirping of the cicadas, I unwound. But it doesn't belong to us. And anyway, Ibiza is crowded, raucous, ruined, with nowhere to walk and the sea full of jellyfish. Even so, this replacement doesn't immediately generate the same emotional response. I know that's inevitable but it still feels a little disappointing.

It's hard to meet, let alone get to know the locals. This is a close farming community, people are withdrawn and very private. Ironically, we have had no callers for five days but just as Joel and Sarah are due to arrive, that changes.

Darty appear right on time with the new electrical goods. This involves not just the installation but a detailed, lengthy explanation and demonstration of how everything works. We are impressed.

'Are you sure they've taken on Comet?' I ask Peter.

The Darty engineers are mid-flow when, to their consternation, the doorbell rings. We excuse ourselves a moment. It's Henri and we need to talk to him – urgently.

We have an invasion of coypu, a family of beaver-like rodents that swim across our lake, eating all vegetation in sight. Henri has already warned us that they have no predator and it falls to us to get rid of them, as their breeding rate is such that they will take over, destroying our trees and digging holes in the sides of the lake.

'So what do we do?' Peter asks.

What you do, he tells us confidently, is buy a cage, put a carrot in it and every time you trap one, hit it hard over the head with a spade.

Peter looks dubious.

'Then you skin it and eat it,' he adds for good measure. '*Ils sont bons.*'

'Really?' I ask, my stomach somersaulting at the very thought.

Well, admits Henri, he has never actually tried one but the locals seem to like them.

The worried expression on Peter's face is becoming semi-permanent. Rural living, it appears, means subscribing to practices he would never normally associate with Christians – namely, the killing of small, furry animals. The thought is distasteful. But he doesn't have time to enquire about alternatives as another visitor arrives, a balding little man, who introduces himself in a high-pitched voice with a slightly complaining edge to it as our near neighbour, Jean Lavale. Henri gets up quickly, sidles past our visitor and, unusually, is out of the front door without so much as a handshake or a backward glance. I leave Monsieur Lavale to Peter, while I give the men from Darty my full attention. If I don't let them finish their erudite spiel, they'll never go.

'That was nice of Monsieur Lavale to call,' I say to Peter, as everyone leaves. 'Our first real visit from a neighbour. No tokens of goodwill, I notice.'

'Don't get too excited,' Peter replies in a low voice. He seems a little paler than he was when I last saw him. 'That was no social call. Apparently he and Henri have been locked in a major legal dispute over the boundaries to our property. He was not at all polite about our predecessor. Worse still, it seems that responsibility for continuing the legal battle has been passed on to us.'

'What does it mean?' I ask, my stomach churning.

'A great deal of money, possibly. I'm not very sure but my heart is in my boots. Legal action is the thing I dreaded more than any other.'

'Why weren't we warned? What do estate agents and solicitors take all that money for?'

Peter shakes his head, baffled. 'Lavale said a very curious thing. He said, "They all pretend to be so proper in this village but behind the façade you wouldn't believe the things that go on here."'

'We don't want to know,' I remind Peter. 'We have enough of that kind of thing at home. We're on sabbatical.'

Monday, 25th September

Joel and Sarah seem to like the place – but I have the nagging feeling that a certain enthusiasm is lacking. It isn't Ibiza, that's for sure. No Mediterranean sea or sun, no spacious bedrooms en suite, no breathtaking view for miles across the bay – and that will take some getting used to. We have all been spoilt.

I have to admit that I never anticipated this emotional disengagement and it makes me feel an ungrateful wretch. I have waited – and saved – all my life for this. Why doesn't it feel more like the dream-come-true it is? I decide to embark on the Hebraic discipline of aiming to find one hundred reasons a day to bless God – an act of will, while my emotions catch up with my brain and mouth.

Number 33 is that we brought plenty of decent paint from England. The French variety, we gather, is the same consistency as skimmed milk and ends up everywhere but on the walls. We spend most of Joel and Sarah's break decorating. It all begins on their first morning when Joel gives a tug at the china blue wallpaper in the sitting room and says, 'I don't think I can live with this a minute longer. Let's just see if it comes off. Hmmm, it does.' After two days of intensive painting that leaves his very pregnant mate in a state of near exhaustion, the sitting room is finally a light and pleasant cream. What will Henri say when he next appears and sees what we have done to what he manifestly thought was the latest fashion look in interior décor, yellow borders and all?

We buy a large cage – big enough for a large rodent – and put it on the far side of the lake with a large, juicy carrot in it. We observe it through binoculars at regular intervals. But thus far, no coypu. Just as well. Had we bagged one, I suspect Peter wouldn't know what to do with it.

Thursday, 28th September

Sarah is assembling dozens of flat packs. Joel has demonstrated how and she turns out to be an expert. I am full of admiration. No matter how many times I watch, I can't get the screws straight. I haven't got the brute strength and it's a source of immense frustration. Why was I made so inadequate? It's not my fault, says creeping self-pity. I take myself in hand. 'So do what you can do and don't lament what you can't.' I cook for everyone.

The local hedgerows are laden with the last blackberries, so I head out with a bucket. Within minutes I realise I'm being watched. Henri and Madeleine's four-year old, who has seen me from the garden of the little cottage that is their temporary home while they decide where they want to live, has let herself out of the gate and crept up behind me.

Chantal eyes me curiously. *'Qu'est-ce que tu fais?'*

Madeleine rushes out and scoops her up in seconds, scolding her both for escaping and for calling me *'tu'* – the familiar form for 'you.' But manifestly, Madeleine is just as intrigued.

'Blackberries,' I explain, 'In England we cook them with apples, then put crumble on top.'

I see I am making no sense at all, so when I get home, I make two blackberry and apple crumbles and take one round to them.

Madeleine accepts it with genuine delight and, to my surprise, tears in her eyes.

'We haven't been able to mix much with our neighbours,' she explains. 'Jealousies.'

I can see she isn't willing to say any more, so I'll leave it.

'Soon, I will bring something special for you,' she shouts after me.

Friday, 29th September

Joel has decided to redesign 'his' kitchen.

'We're not dead yet,' Peter reminds him wryly.

One of the joys of working on a house that doesn't need anything doing to it is that it's never exactly how you want it and what you do do has to be done without destroying what didn't need doing. The kitchen is actually a disaster. The cooker, crowned with a cooker hood that Henri has just installed with a flue through the ceiling above, is wedged into a corner and I have to cook with my nether regions pressed against a cupboard. The wall cupboards are so low over the sink that no one can see the dishes they are washing. There are no matching counters and hardly any electric sockets. Nothing, we discover, as Peter leans on a cupboard and lands on the floor on top of the pieces, is fitted. Probably just as well. But how do we rectify the situation without ruining the pretty tiles and pleasant decoration?

The men set to. It looks like major building works and I want to cry. But Joel does an amazing job. Up in the loft he discovers that the flue was actually blowing cooker muck straight into the attic, so he creates a proper exit. Then he cuts a new hole in the kitchen ceiling where we need it and fits the plaster board circle he removes exactly into the old hole. It's meticulous work and his feathers are easily ruffled.

'Push the tube up, Dad,' he shouts down into the kitchen with exasperation. 'What's wrong with you? You're miles away from the hole.'

'I can't see any more, that's why,' his dad replies. Peter mutters to me, 'Why don't youngsters understand what happens to your body with the passage of time?'

Then Joel replaces the tiles he has hacked out, to his immense annoyance slightly cracking one in the process – but only one: pins back new strips of beading and matches a piece of wallpaper to the bare plaster with such artistry that when the job is finished, only someone who knew what had been done could tell. He finishes the job by cleaning seven years of fat off the newly exposed tiles. What a well brought-up child he is. Later, too late, we find a spare tile, just like the cracked one, in the cellar.

This is straightforward: the rest of the project is not. All of the cupboards are different heights and depths – none are standard. We have bought brand new melamine counter tops. They are not standard either and none of them fit. Even the sockets are not European standard. Welcome to France. Not only that but we soon discover that the wallpaper, called in French *'papier peint'* – is indeed painted paper. The tiniest wipe washes the pattern off.

We move cupboards around, cut off their bottoms, extend their backs, cut out matching counter tops, all different widths, drag wires from sockets elsewhere, polyfill holes in tiles and carry on patching up the wallpaper. Despite some very unspiritual noises that accompany the hacking, banging, sawing and pasting, there is a real satisfaction in seeing a fitted kitchen spring to life for just a few euros. As long as no one looks too closely.

The doorbell rings. It's Henri and Madeleine with an offering, as promised. I wonder how they will feel when they see what we have done with the kitchen. Thankfully, they are genuinely impressed.

'Why didn't we think of this, Henri?' Madeleine asks, as she lifts the tea towel off a large serving dish. Underneath is a plateful of snails.

My stomach lurches at the sight.

'You collect blackberries from our bushes and I collect snails – from your gate,' she says. 'And I filled them with a *farcie* – garlic butter. *J'adore ça.*'

I try to look grateful. She senses my hesitation.

'Anyway, I leave them with you,' she says graciously.

After they've gone we all sit looking at the dish. Peter is the first to reach out a hand and take one. He inserts a cocktail stick, pulls out the meat and pops it into his mouth.

'This is what missionaries have to do,' he tells us.

We watch his face. It's inscrutable.

'The sauce is nice,' he says, the butter dripping down his chin.

There's no sudden dash for the loo and since I'm determined to respect Madeleine's generosity, I slowly put one into my mouth too, trying hard not to breathe through my nose. It's just like eating a piece of rubber – tasteless but for the garlic. I can't bring myself to eat any more. Being a missionary has its limits.

Saturday, 30th September

On their last night the children take us to our first real French restaurant right by the river in Montmorillon. It's what my Jewish sister-in-law would call fancy-*schmanzy*. The waitress has to explain the menu in detail – and that was for the French. I had so hoped for a *tarte tatin* or a *tarte au citron* but there was Spotty Dick instead and they manifestly thought it very avant garde. I gave the snails and frogs' legs a very wide berth.

During dessert Joel has a coughing fit. He's spent days in the loft fighting his way through fibreglass but the icing sugar has finally got his throat.

Almost a week – and still no coypu in our cage.

October

Any attempt at theological study has been severely hampered by lengthy negotiations to get an online facility, an electricity account and a bank that will allow us to withdraw more than the equivalent of £200 a week. We are fast running out of cheques, with no new cheque-book in sight and starvation looms ever closer, while our Toy Town Post Office bank appears to fiddle with the money we deposited before we came. This is not conducive to a stress-free existence and there is much regular, slow breathing on our part. It's beginning to feel too much like life at home.

I have promised *The Church of England Newspaper* a diary of our sabbatical and would like to send it to them before we arrive back, so we ring France Telecom daily. It has apparently been taken over by Orange, which has a monopoly of virtually the entire world but not the staff to cope with it. There is the now all-too-familiar response to any call: 'Press one if . . ., Press two if . . ., Press three . . .', on and on through six options. Unlike in the UK, you cannot interrupt the process at any point and it takes a full two minutes and eleven seconds. We timed it. When you finally get through a voice says, 'Please tap in the ten digits of your phone number.' That done, the voice says, 'Please tap in the ten digits of your reference number.' Then you wait for around another two minutes, to be told, nine times out of ten, 'Sorry, all our consultants are busy, please ring back another time,' and are cut off. Unless you call accounts, in which case someone responds instantly. When you do get through, a human voice says, *'Bonjour*, could I have your telephone number? And now your reference number?'

'We've already tapped them in,' Peter says, with admirable self-control.

'Your telephone and reference number, Monsieur?' repeats the voice.

Peter capitulates. 'You sent us a broadband package. I have installed it but it still won't work. You told me eight days ago I would be connected in seven days.'

'Ah, Monsieur, seven days is entirely theoretical – a notional time.'

Finally, a euro seems to drop and a hint of warmth comes into the voice, 'Aren't you the Englishman I spoke to yesterday? And where did you say you live, Monsieur? Out in the countryside? You'll never get broadband there, not yet at least. You'll have to have dial-up.'

'That's what I thought – but your colleagues assured me I'd get broadband. And how long will it take to get dial-up?'

'A few hours, Monsieur.'

She explains the process. We've been trying ever since, without success.

We finally unpacked the last box today – books inevitably but the irony was that having got them out at last, I couldn't settle to reading any of them and wandered around the house restlessly looking for something to do. It wasn't difficult. We have been besieged by a ferocious plague of flies, apparently affecting the whole village – to our relief – otherwise the rural life might have lost its appeal before it barely began. We are trying a variety of methods of eco-kindly pest control that involves sticking patches of sex hormones to the windows. Not being very *au fait* with the mating habits of the common fly, I am at a loss to know quite how they work. Suffice it to say that hundreds are lying helplessly on their backs all over our verandah floor in various positions of what may well be the equivalent of post-coital bliss, while I spoil the fun with my vacuum cleaner.

Study, said the Hebrew sages, is the highest form of worship. God welcomes obedience as a reflection of our deepest love. We have to know what he wants before we can obey. And knowing comes from studying his word. So it bothers me that when faced with the opportunity, I so often revert to stereotypical, obsessional Jewish house-wife mode. Out with the feather duster! This hyperactiv-ity isn't just a reflection of the stressful past fortnight – the inevitable companion of buying and setting up a new home. For as long as I can remember I have avoided any form of retreat, using a busy working life in the NHS as my excuse. And now, having lost the ability to be still, I don't know how to find it again. Study and quiet reflec-tion require time and dedication. Discipline is vital but whether willpower alone can control a mind as restless as the North Sea remains to be seen.

Monday, 2nd October

I have done the unthinkable – dead-headed the roses without wearing gloves. Last night the middle finger on my right hand swelled up like a pork banger and began to throb. I couldn't remove my grandmother's gold wedding ring and had to swallow a rising panic that the circulation would stop, the finger turn black and fall off. I spent the entire night checking it was still there.

This morning I take myself off to the local village pharmacist. '*Hein*!' she comments, holding the sausage up to the light, 'you've been gardening. When did you last have a tetanus injection?' I say I think it was six years ago but can't be sure. 'Then you must see a doctor. I can't offer you anything. Last time I had one like this they had to cut off her . . .' I feel faint with relief when she finally adds 'ring' – not that I'd be too happy to forego a family heirloom.

There is only one doctor in the village. As it happens, says the pharmacist, pointing across the road, I'm fortunate, his surgery is open. He takes appointments on Monday mornings, visits Monday afternoons and holds open surgery on Wednesday and Friday afternoons. On Tuesdays and Thursdays, he's in Limoges, helping Jehovah's Witnesses avoid blood transfusions.

I take my place in the unmarked waiting room at the back of the doctor's brand new house on the edge of the village. Four or five longsuffering patients already there alternately lament their own decrepit state or the equally decrepit state of the health services in France. There is no receptionist, no one to let the doctor know I'm here and, since it's Monday morning, more and more people keep arriving, announcing the time of their appointment as they do, so I am continually relegated to the back of the queue. Each appointment seems to take around fifteen minutes, so I realise I could be here all day. At least the conversation is entertaining.

After around an hour and a half or so, I urgently need to spend a penny and am directed through the door that leads to the doctor's surgery. His glass door, through which I can see and hear a very private consultation, is on the left, the loo door is on the right. There is no sink in it, nor can I find anywhere to wash my hands. This is the norm in most French homes but I'm shocked to find that the doctor isn't hygiene-conscious either.

Eventually, when I take my seat in the waiting-room again, a sour-faced woman who arrived some 45 minutes after I did takes pity on me and whispers 'Go in straight after me. And don't let anyone know you have no appointment.'

She's being kind-hearted, she says, because she likes the English. She's from Paris and no one in the village likes her. They all treat her as an outsider – except the English, who are not aware of local prejudices.

What does one do here in an emergency, I ask. She and the one remaining patient, an elderly man with a very flushed face, laugh. 'You dial 15 but don't expect anything to happen.' The nearest intensive care unit is in Limoges, over an hour away by car. 'They take you by helicopter,' says the elderly man. 'That happened to me six months ago. Heart.' He beats his chest with his fist and coughs.

'What was it like?'

'I don't know. I was too ill to know what was happening.'

'Don't even bother dialling 15,' says the happy Parisienne, apparently especially if it's a child. 'Just bundle them into a car and take them to the hospital in Montmorillon.'

'Thirty minutes away?' I gasp. 'That could be twenty five too late.'

'There's no A and E,' she adds for good measure, 'but they won't turn you away. I've done it at least three times.'

A raft of potentially dire emergencies pass in technicolour through my mind – especially with a first new grandchild on the way – and I pray silently and earnestly that none of them happen.

Finally, the Parisienne has her turn, which seems to take an inordinate amount of time. As she leaves I leap up before anyone else and follow the doctor the moment he has seen her simpering presence off the premises.

He is sympathetic and efficient, even if he has no idea what's wrong with the finger. He sends me out with a prescription for a strong anti-inflammatory and tells me to come back quickly if there is no improvement in a couple of days. No major surgery yet then. That's a relief. As is the lack of a bill.

I can think of better ways of spending an entire day than being in a tiny waiting room. Although one does see life.

Tuesday, 3rd October

I suddenly realise today that part of my surprising lack of pleasure in my new home is the fear deep down that we have made a terrible mistake. There's the tiniest niggle buried somewhere in my brain that keeps saying, 'All that money you've blown – a lifetime of savings – might you not have found something better?' That kind of thinking, I now see, leads nowhere. In fact, it ends in dissatisfaction and disappointment – the general malaise of most of British society. What sort of a God do I have? To my shame, despite all I preach to others, I fear he may be a niggling, withholding fake of my own creation, rather than the loving, generous reality he is. I have to accept that though it was a leap of faith, we were clear when we bought the house that this was where we were meant to be and what was right then must be right now. Therein lies peace of mind and a grateful spirit.

This welcome revelation has been facilitated by Dave and Meriel, our church co-ordinator and his wife, who arrived yesterday in our car. They'll stay for a week, then take the van home.

Meriel takes a wonderful, child-like pleasure in every-thing – the peaceful view, the burgundy bathroom tiles, even the kitchen cupboards. She is fascinated by HyperU – the French supermarket – and finds all kinds of treats I have missed – mini pizzas, chipsters, cran-berry and pepper Boursin cheese, almond pear pie. Through her eyes I am beginning to see so many small pleasures I seem to have missed or taken for granted. Why have I been walking around with my eyes shut?

She didn't like the bright orange of the rustic, rough plaster of the huge downstairs room, I'm glad to say, as neither did we and now, with a great deal of effort and commitment on the part of our guests, the walls are slowly turning cream. Our house is what the French call a *pavillon*, a bungalow on stilts with a garage beneath, the entire size of the house. Our predecessor has already divided it in two and created a large extra sitting room or games room – large enough to seat around thirty peo-ple, should an urge to church plant ever surface. Now, instead of being a dismal, artificially-lit, dayglo expanse, it's light and pleasant.

For respite, we take them to our local for the menu du jour. It's too cold to sit out, we are informed, before we had even considered where to sit – probably because Madame La Patronne can't be bothered walking a few extra metres for a few mad English – and we are ushered with the usual, unsmiling formality into a dingy back room with worn vinyl flooring, imitation dark wood walls, yellowing wallpaper and oil paintings manifestly bought from street vendors. The meal makes up for the lack of décor – five courses of home-cooked French food. Around thirty workmen, reduced to silence as men are when their bellies are filled with good food and wine, wipe the sweat off their brow and mop their plates with gusto. If they're surprised to be joined by four, obviously non-labouring English, they don't show it. But then, they have more passing preoccupations.

The finger shows minimal improvement. Thanks to copious soaking in cold water, soap and hand cream, not to mention Meriel's earnest prayers and my stoicism in the face of great pain, Peter manages to remove the ring, so the sausage is no longer constricted at the base. That's a huge psychological relief.

Still no coypu in our cage. Why are they giving us the cold shoulder? At least Orange now loves us. We finally have dial-up.

Wednesday, 4th–Thursday, 5th October

The weather is frighteningly atrocious. So much for the autumn idyll we anticipated. Torrential rainstorms lash our fields. We stand on our verandah and watch the lake rise and overflow its banks, gouging a full-bodied, rush-ing river right through the middle of our land. It looks as if it's going to destroy all the shrubs and hedges and sweep our garden away in its wake.

'What's happened to the coypu cage?' I ask Peter.

'Still there,' he says, identifying it through the binoculars.

'With any luck the flood will sweep the little beasts away too.'

I have visions of them floating past on top of the cage, their worldly belongings with them – TV, bedding, fridge, kids – looking for a new abode.

Over the next two days, like Noah and his wife, we watch and wait as the waters slowly recede, revealing the prostrate form of a 350-year old oak tree. The dam-age could have been a great deal worse but we grieve for this lovely chunk of history.

'The coypu,' Henri says grimly, pointing at the tree, when he comes round to confirm with evident satisfaction that the house he has built has weathered the elements.

'Do we sell the wood?' Peter asks sadly.

Henri shrugs. 'You can but it's hardly worth it.'

Coypu and badgers apparently have a total disregard for history. With so many dead trees around, oak is simply used as firewood. And oh no, the flood hasn't seen our unadopted new pets off. Even as we speak, a family swims nonchalantly past us, frolicking in the new increased expanse of leisure facilities.

Friday, 6th October

We are determined to plant lots of new trees – a forest, in fact, in one of our fields – which will remove the huge worry of mowing it, if nothing else. It is both an oppressing and salutary thought that it will be our grandchildren and great grandchildren who will enjoy the benefits. Oppressing, because the reality of the ageing process forces me to confront the loss of the gift I have only just been given. Salutary in that I must recognise that the house, the land and its trees will long outlive me and therefore never be truly mine. Perhaps this is why having my own home hasn't brought quite the satisfaction I thought it would. In all these years of ministry, I have been a rather restless soul and put it down to rootlessness, the not-knowing where we would spend our retirement. But perhaps my restlessness has been spiritual rather than physical. On this earth we are gone so quickly. How can we ever put our roots down? 'We are being prepared for our eternal destination – a city that's yet to come,' said the writer to the Hebrew Church. We disappear and the land goes on without us. That's why we can never truly own it. All we have is a temporary stewardship that brings huge responsibility – and anxiety.

Theologian Walter Brueggemann, in his fascinating book *The Land*, which Peter is studying, claims that the Children of Israel never realised how totally unencumbered they were in the wilderness. God provided for all their needs. They had no concerns. But the moment they became landowners their problems began. Soil, like gold, worms its way into our hearts and creates its own peculiar possessiveness. It can be a curse that makes neighbours feud, that barricades Englishmen into their 'castles' and condemns people to years of war, as it has in the Middle East. Or it can be a garden to cultivate as it was at the beginning of time, a paradise for all to share. Whichever, it does bring worry, as we are beginning to discover, as we wonder how we will ever tend such a large area from so far away. I do hope we have done the right thing.

As I reflect, I find it interesting that so many ministers feel it isn't worth improving their homes and gardens. 'It's not mine,' they say. 'No point in doing anything to it since it brings no capital gain.' But surely, like any rented property, a tied house is as much our responsibility as a house that belongs to us? Am I not my brother's keeper, with a duty to my successors?

Saturday, 7th October

I have, *par chance*, in my attempt to have read the entire Bible before our sabbatical comes to an end, reached the dreaded books of Chronicles – not the most promising of texts for meditation, I thought. Yet how wrong could I be. Chronicling has always been important for the Jewish people. Knowing our past enables us to come to terms with the present and plan wisely for the future. King David was forced to face the fact that, as a man of war, he would never have peace for long enough to fulfil his lifelong ambition to build a magnificent Temple in Jerusalem. So he left everything in place and ready for his son to do it. Perhaps it isn't foolish, so late in life and with so few resources, to invest in a property we hope will be a source of rest and pleasure to friends, family and tired, jaded Christians for years to come.

I was more hard pressed to understand how that son, Solomon, a man of such supposed wisdom, could have been so naive in matters of state, imposing centralised bureaucracy, heavy taxation, conscription and institutionalised religion – all the heavy-handedness of authority that would undermine and eventually undo the stability of government and nation for future generations. But Solomon didn't only have wisdom, he had everything else as well – mouth-watering material wealth, status and power and, somewhere along the way, the man drowned in the trappings of his success. The more he had, the more he thought he needed. He became acquisitive and proprietorial, prone to show and exaggeration. His own house was even bigger than God's Temple. He had the equivalent of three wives and concubines a day (what man can reasonably cope with more than one?) and a vast army with the latest tools of war to protect his land. Here was a very real warning about the dangers of property and prosperity.

It's hard to believe that a man who had intimate access to so many women could have written the Song of Songs, the great love song that is ascribed to him. I prefer the theory that it was written by the opposition –

a young man with a broken heart whose love was snatched away by his abusive monarch. After all, Solomon himself was the progeny of a king who had fancied the wife of one of his footsoldiers and taken her because he could. And history has a tendency to repeat itself, a lesson few of us seem to consider before we fall headlong into some of our most senseless acts. Whether this was true of Solomon or not, flattery and fawning appears to have gone to his head and curdled his spiritual senses. It's an object lesson in loss of vision and very apposite for us here in France. Solomon's children inherited his empire but never really appreciated the gift, as they had lost sight of the Giver.

Our '*château*' may not have historic charm or rustic cottage appeal, with its Quickfix doors and taps, its twelve square metre bedrooms and Legoland kitchen but it is enough for us. What we must do is save and plant as many trees as we can and that means tackling the coypu problem.

'There's one in the cage,' Peter announces, as he comes in from the garden, breathless. With surprise or anxiety, I'm not sure.

'Go for it, wild man,' I encourage my hunter gatherer. After all, the writer John Eldredge is selling books on the basis that men need a manly adventure.

He looks unsure. 'I don't think Henri has ever killed a coypu. I can't see how to get a spade through the cage bars. A spike might do the trick.'

Can he bring himself to kill an animal the size of a large cat? Maybe he'll just try France Telecom one more time instead – or perhaps the bank. Or perhaps he'll put together yet another flat-pack wardrobe. Surely that's masculine adventure enough for one day?

But then there's the fallen oak. We don't want any more of them.

'What did you do?' I ask, as he returns, grey in the face and shaking.

Never have I felt so like Lady Macbeth.

'Drowning. They're not afraid of water. It seemed the kindest way.'

Whatever the future when we return to England, a rural parish is never going to suit us.

Monday, 9th October

It's our last day with the van and that means another trip to Limoges. The last bed base has arrived today – at the very last minute. But still no wardrobe from Atlas. Not sure how we will manage to balance it on a car when it does arrive.

There are last lamps, mirrors and rugs to be bought – and, most important of all, a lawn mower. We just 'pop' into Soury Jardin on the way home, so that my engineering husband can ogle at a shop full of mouth-watering gadgets – saws and strimmers and trimmers. Each has to be demonstrated, examined and fondled. The owner is in his element sharing what almost sound like pornographic pleasures with such a discerning customer. This is France after all. And I haven't even brought a book to read.

By the time Peter makes up his mind, the owner has been called away to rescue his elderly father who has been out mushroom picking and whose Citroen 2 CV has got stuck in the middle of a field. The lesser salespeople have no idea what kind of deal has been struck, cannot help and have no idea when he will be back. Perhaps Monsieur had better take Madame for *an aperitif* at the café over the road, they suggest, eyeing me nervously. But finding himself in paradise, *Monsieur* cannot be easily torn away. Three hours later we finally load the equipment into the van, Peter with boyish excitement, I with tight lips and a sour expression.

Our last supper with Dave and Meriel has been ready for two hours. They are more forgiving than I am. But then, they don't have to share his affections with machinery.

Tuesday, 10th October

Now that all visitors have gone home, I am finding it very hard to come to terms with being alone. Here is a golden opportunity to devote myself to prayer and reflection but do I do it? Does the moon revolve around the sun? I'm not sure why we all have those times when God seems a thousand miles away and his voice as remote as the curlew's call in Oxford Street. I just hope he turns up before we go home.

I bicycle into the village to the local *boulangerie* for our baguettes – a five mile round trip. This has to beat cycling of the stationary variety in our cellar at home in front of daytime TV. The views are so much nicer.

Once there I hang around in the square for a while, longing to meet someone, anyone . . . which is a bit sad. I remind myself of the childhood me, going off alone for long bike rides on our local trading estate, because I couldn't think of what else to do. I study adverts in shop windows, read posters on lamp posts, sit on benches looking friendly. But the weather is turning too cool for passing the time of day. And what Frenchman or woman who has lived here all their life wants to meet yet another English incomer, who probably barely speaks their language?

I look out for the familiar fish symbol on a car – sure that one must appear one day, mustn't it? Where are these Christians? Where are they hiding?

Wednesday, 11th October

If the neighbours won't come to you, you have to go to the neighbours.

We set off into the commune with determination and call at the first open door, a mere one hundred yards or so from our house. A tinny-sounding doorbell plays *Frère Jacques* and a weary, rather bedraggled old lady in a quilted pink dressing gown wrapped around her more than ample girth shuffles out to us, a quizzical expression on her face.

'We're your new neighbours,' Peter says brightly.

'Ah, excuse me,' she says, 'I'm so ill, always ill but come in anyway.'

We follow her into a dark, pokey little house, which she rents from Monsieur Lavale, she tells us. As our eyes become accustomed to the gloom, we see that it manifestly hasn't had any loving attention for many years. In what looks like a 1950s scullery she points us to a table in a dining area, covered in patterned oil cloth and piled high with books, papers and other debris. We sit and, with competition from a very noisy budgie, hear a long medical history of back pain, diabetes, haemophilia and urinary infections. Peter, I notice, is nodding sympathetically, back in pastoral mode. We manage, finally, to elicit that her name is Marguerite.

The district nurse arrives to give Marguerite her daily injection.

'My new neighbours,' she announces proudly, waving in our direction as if we're old friends. 'They live in the *joli chalet*.'

So that's what the locals call our house.

'At least they speak French,' says the nurse damply, as we greet her and get up to go.

Marguerite insists we stay.

'Oh yes, I see it all, believe me,' the nurse says, as she takes a clean needle out of its packet and inserts it in the syringe. 'These English, can't understand a word I say most of the time. How can I explain what the drugs are for? When there's a couple, they seem to think they can get away with only one of them speaking French – usually the man,' she adds dismissively. Dependency in a woman is evidently not her style.

'The rumour round here is that you're a pastor,' Marguerite says to Peter after the nurse has packed up her things and taken her leave with a curt nod of the head. 'What kind of pastor?'

Peter tries to explain but Church of England means nothing in France. Marguerite says she's *evangeliste*. Do we understand what that is? We finally elucidate, to our amazement, that she used to belong to a Pentecostal church, the Assemblies of God, before she moved to this area. 'So where do you worship now?' we ask her.

She shakes her head sadly. There is nowhere, she says, no assembly within a hour's drive. She has not met another Christian who shares her convictions for at least seven years. This is a depressing thought. I tell her I'm convinced there must be some meeting nearer than that and it's just a case of finding them. But she simply smiles at me indulgently.

Peter suddenly notices a large, dog-eared Bible on the table, half-hidden beneath mounds of newspaper clippings and discarded tissues.

'Would you like us to read some Scripture and pray with you?' Peter offers.

She nods enthusiastically. He has evidently proved he has the right credentials. 'I haven't prayed with anyone for such a very long time.' She weeps copiously as he does so, blowing her nose loudly between lots of 'Amens.'

We finally wrench ourselves away – after many demands to come back soon, a barrage of kissing and exclamations about the goodness of God.

'After all these years, God has finally answered my prayers,' she calls after us down the road.

'A flippin' expensive way for God to do it – it cost us a house,' I mutter to Peter as we walk back home, leaving Marguerite exclaiming behind us how wonderful it is to have her own pastor at last. My heart sinks.

Thursday, 12th October

Marguerite confirmed yesterday that she doesn't find the locals friendly and this, we discover to our dismay, is due in part to prolonged legal battles between our predecessor and his neighbours. Peter's informant, Monsieur Lavale, whose land borders on our eastern side, is utterly convinced that Henri is a charlatan who has been encroaching on his territory, centimetre by centimetre, moving a boundary that his grandfather clearly delineated for him when he was a child. Not only that but Henri has been inflicting damage on his property, chopping down his trees and razing hedges to the ground. This is why he intends to sue him but before he can do so, the boundaries, set in the Napoleonic era, have to be formally established by the local court.

Ironically, while Peter is out, an official letter is delivered to our door by the court administrator in person, instructing Peter to attend a tribunal later in the month. I have to sign to say I have received it.

'What does it mean?' I ask Peter as I hand him the letter.

'It means this is serious stuff. Lavale claims when he confronted Henri with the matter, Henri raised his fist and would have landed one on him, had he not made a quick getaway.'

'That's a bit shocking. But I can't believe it of Henri.'

'There's certainly evidence of some malevolence – tree stumps and huge gaps in the hedgerow.'

Now we see how right Walter Brueggeman is. Land ownership can be costly, robbing the spirit of its peace. If we thought a house in France would provide sanctuary from reality, we were under a sad illusion. There is no escaping difficult relationships, stressful situations and personal responsibilities. According to Abbot Christopher Jamison of Worth Abbey, whose book, *Finding Sanctuary* is my spiritual food at the moment, learning to walk through the minefield of life with integrity is the door to the respite we long for: an inner spiritual space.

Unknowingly, Father Jamison is helping me come to terms with feeling under par, unable to enter fully into the gift we have been given – both the place itself and the time to enjoy it. Since I gave up a senior management job in communications in the NHS, I have felt restless and dissatisfied. My lack of DIY ability and the resulting inevitable dependence on Peter has compounded my frustrations. I feel de-skilled. Even the daily trip to the village by bike for fresh bread, such fun at first, has lost its lustre and novelty. I feel reduced to being a housewife and despite speaking French, fear I am becoming the kind of woman despised by the district nurse.

I suspect I may be experiencing withdrawal symptoms. Over the years I have developed an addiction to busyness and can't cope without the adrenaline rush it gives me. If the house was only a consumerist dream, if that was all that drove me to work so hard all these years to save the capital, it would and could be no antidote to my addiction. I am not sure what is. The key to discovering the inner sanctuary Father Jamison says we all search for and need, eludes me at the moment. But perhaps Marguerite's prayers, drawing us here, do have a part to play. I shall hold onto that for the time being.

Friday, 13th October

Today I had my first real conversation with the young woman who owns the Spar. I told her that yesterday I lost the magnificent cauliflower she had sold me. It was balanced in a plastic bag on my handle bars and must have fallen off on the way home. I went back almost at once but no sign of it and there were tire marks in the mud at the most likely spot.

'Someone obviously needs that cauliflower more than you,' she suggests.

'We managed very well with the tinned sweetcorn instead.'

She looks dubious. 'Just not the same thing,' she sympathises.

I buy plums and explain I'm going to top it with a crumble, which is pastry English-style – left in bits.

'Ah yes,' she says enthusiastically, 'I know crumble. I love it. I make it with strawberries and put chunks of chocolate on top.'

I nod uncertainly. This doesn't sound like any crumble I recognise. Nor am I sure about the strawberry and chocolate mix. But I'm not going to end the relationship when it has barely started by arguing about crumble.

At home the phone rings. A woman representing a company tendering for the swimming pool that Peter's brother is so kindly making it possible for us to build wants to know when it will be convenient to call. Her name is Aurelie Moreau. I don't realise what a mouthful that is for anyone not used to rolling their r's and find myself saying, 'Ah, *bonjour* Madame Orelly.' I realise that isn't right and say at once, 'Non, bonjour Madame Morelly.' In acute embarrassment, I hear myself saying, 'I'll get my husband.' The coward's way out!

Sunday, 15th October

Peter insists on keeping Sunday special despite the fact that we have still not managed to locate a church. I resent it. Isn't every day a Sabbath here? I had quickly made up my mind that unless Peter DIY-ed every day, we would never get everything done in twelve weeks.

He has a different approach. 'Today is Sunday,' he announces, 'so all the chores that need doing will just have to wait.'

As it happens, it's a glorious day and as we bike through little French villages in the peaceful countryside, I begin to understand that Sabbath is a gift, not an imposition. The Jews say it is a taste of heaven. And that is exactly how it feels today, with the wind in my hair and the sun on my face. I feel revitalised and, when we arrive home, rested.

I decide to do a little study on the subject and am fascinated by what I discover. Sabbath isn't only about rest. It has wider implications. Having one day a week when we neither work nor employ others to work for us, when we neither buy nor sell, when we let the land be, creates a new world order where all the hierarchies of power and wealth, all the injustices and inequalities of the workplace and free market, are temporarily put on hold. It is a reminder that we are creations, not just creators with absolute control of our universe. We cannot go on endlessly exploiting it and those who live in it and expect to survive intact. And if we cannot let go of our urges for power and control one day in seven, then we are seriously and dangerously out of emotional and spiritual kilter. 'Human freedom is expressed as much in the ability to stop as in the ability to work,' says the Chief Rabbi, Jonathan Sacks. Coming to a deliberate standstill every week demonstrates that we can be the masters, not the slaves of our busyness.

Sabbath was a gift at creation – ignored at our peril. In the book of Exodus it becomes a vital aspect of the covenant relationship between God and the people he loves so much, that he wants their undivided attention one day a week – a 'holy' sanctuary in time, for stillness and reflection. It may well be the key to my deliverance from the unholy drivenness that so often motivates my actions. After all, we are in the midst of a three-month Sabbath – and I baulked at the thought of a single day's recreation.

The Book of Genesis says that God placed human beings in the Garden of Eden 'to work it and take care of it.' The Hebrew word translated 'to take care of' suggests only temporary guardianship. Here I am, face to face yet again with this notion of our being trustees for future generations. We don't own the world. Sabbath is a weekly opportunity to live that reality.

I am fascinated to discover that the Hebrew Bible con-
tains some of the world's earliest environmental legislation. Don't destroy trees under the pretext of war, says
the book of Deuteronomy. Let fields lie fallow once in
seven years, commands Leviticus. Several other prohibi-
tions which have always mystified me – such as the
command not to mix milk and meat or to sow mixed
grain – are in fact symbolic. They are warnings that
remind human beings to respect the integrity of nature.
I notice that each life form has its part to play in the
earth's complex ecology. Oooops! What about killing
coypu? These decisions are so difficult. And then I see it
for the first time – a command to honour your neighbours' boundaries. The boundaries of the promised
land, the inheritance of the ancient Children of Israel
who were dramatically rescued from slavery in Egypt
and set out into the desert to look for a homeland, are
proscribed in detail, on every side. What's more, the
ancient laws are tough on people who try to enlarge
their boundaries at the cost of their neighbour, especially if that neighbour is unable to defend themselves. In
other words, in a just community, unfair acquisition of
land is totally condemned.

Perhaps I should be a little more sympathetic to
Monsieur Lavale's obsession with his boundaries. But in
this case who has been unjust – Henri or Lavale? We
won't know until the court establishes where the boundaries are. And then, apparently, justice will be done.

Monday, 16th October

I'm gradually feeling less unsettled by the curdling mix
of the lack of familiar routine, loss of status and vague

homesickness. I realised things had come to a sorry pass at the end of last week when I caught myself saying, 'This cycling into the village for fresh bread every day is such a pain (if French-speakers will pardon the pun) – bring back the stodgy, preservative-laden stuff that lasts a week at home.' I am now consciously making the trip an opportunity for reflection. Repeating various phrases such as, 'Be still and know that I am God,' in time with my breathing pattern, focuses the mind and wards off distractions.

I find myself yawning a lot and actually sleep eight hours a night, having prided myself for years that I only needed six. I thought I was achieving more by sleeping less but have probably been working with rather more limited concentration than I realised. There's no escaping the fact that I have tended to value myself by jobs done – and am beginning to realise that this is a useful pre-retirement insight. I could never have been a minister – ending every day with mounds of waiting paperwork, unfinished projects and unsorted out people.

Perhaps that's why Peter has found it easier to settle here from the start. He has had to come to terms with all the untied ends of his daily routine and will return to them soon enough. I suspect that it's also because the emotional and social needs of men are less demanding, more focused on the one-stop, all-sufficient spouse. Carpentry and gardening appear to be adequate compensation too. Hobbies have been a rare luxury in his relentless, six-day week. The one day-off is so filled with the essentials of existence – paying the bills, mowing the grass and mending endless breakages – that the creative occupations he once loved have been totally neglected. As I watch him re-discover the joys of physical labour and exhaustion, I realise with a catch in my throat just how much his work has cost him, how much is lost.

But then, most people are caught up in this madness. It seems I may have been unfair in my assumptions of why the English come here. It's not just the lure of the climate and cheap housing but because of a rather depressing view of what life in Britain has become. Our English estate agent pops in and brings Paul, an electrical engineer, who left five businesses and two coronaries behind. He says he couldn't take any more theft, break-ins, hidden cameras, long traffic queues, rising fuel costs, unrealistic customer expectations, lack of safety for the kids and non-existent family time. Why have we allowed such an erosion of the quality of our national life, I wonder. The French would have been out on the streets, protesting with barricades. Have we simply lost sight of any alternative?

Not that *la vie française* is perfect. Paul admitted that he has double the paperwork for only one business here, compared to the five he ran in England. But the compensations are worth it. He loves shutting down for a two hour lunch-break every day – and stalwartly sticks to it, even though it makes his English clients howl.

On Sundays only the biggest supermarkets open – for two hours in the morning to sell fresh bread. Cafés and restaurants serve the traditional all-day Sunday lunch to large, extended family gatherings but have to close on Mondays. A day off is statutory in France. Our *boulangerie* is open on Sundays and Mondays but closed on Wednesdays. On Wednesdays schools are closed half day for sport. On Saturdays there are variable closures. It's amazing any work gets done at all. We're still waiting for the wardrobe from Atlas we ordered five weeks ago and that, they tell us, is nothing, madame.

On the other hand, if the French can have one day a week for family, why can't we? The 'Keep Sunday Special' campaign might have succeeded, had not businesses convinced the government that opening shops on Sundays would boost national profits. Company directors couldn't see that they and their workforce needed one sacrosanct day off.

The favourite leisure time pursuit, when the locals are not eating, is hunting – wild boar, rabbits, deer, pheasants, anything that moves. Self-discipline is not enough of a national characteristic to sustain health and safety measures, so not a week goes by without another hunting misadventure in the news. Last week the victim was a farmer's wife who was taking her husband the packed lunch he had inadvertently left behind. Perhaps he'd asked for tuna, and she's brought him cheese. Local mayors are desperately trying to opening up ramblers' paths, barbwired off by gun-toting farmers – to little purpose, it seems, if any unsuspecting walker can be mowed down in a hail of bullets.

Henri loathes hunting, he tells me, as he tries to herd his beautiful chestnut-brown Limousin cows out of our field. He takes them for a walk every day. Exercise, he explains, wards off cow bronchitis. But he can't get them to adapt to a change of direction.

'Once they get into the habit . . .' he apologises with some embarrassment, flailing his arms and shouting, '*Venez, venez*' – to no great effect.

'Tradition!' I commiserate. 'Like humans.' I know about that. I'm Jewish and an Anglican.

'This urge to kill things is a disgrace', he claims, as he finally steers them back along the path.

'Coypu?' I ask.

'Different,' he shouts back, then adds, with a wink, 'Never actually done it.'

No wonder he isn't popular with the neighbours. Not when the goat farmer next door to us happens to be the President of the local hunt.

I run out of flour and make a special trip into the village, by bike, to find the Spar is closed. An assistant packing shelves points to the sign outside. It says, 'We're open 24/7' and in small print underneath 'but not between midday and 2 pm, not after 6pm and not Sunday afternoons or Mondays.'

October 17th

Marguerite rings, ostensibly with lists of churches – in reality angling for a visit. I comply. After all, she is the only neighbour I know as yet and it's a great opportunity to work on my French. When she opens the door, she is still in her dressing gown.

This time, woman to woman, she is much more forthcoming and tells me about her strange domestic arrangements. It appears she is married but not married. Bruno, her second husband, who at sixty-two is ten years her junior, ran off with a thirty-five year old a year ago. Her three children were all fathered by her first husband, a haemophiliac who bled to death when he was only thirty-three after a drunken night club brawl. She sniffs. He had it coming but left her penniless. She ran a market stall to support her children, then met Bruno, a farm labourer who brought her to the area in the hope of finding work. He has always treated the children as his own, so despite his perfidy and betrayal, because of their affection for him and because of her beliefs, she will not divorce him. Instead, they are legally separated. French law, she explains, requires that they see each other every day and care for each other if necessary. It all sounds very odd to me. Given her uncertain state of health, he comes to check on her every lunchtime and she cooks him a meal. Convenient, then.

She repeatedly says, 'Oh la la, la la, la la' in a very deep voice at the back of her throat, which gives her thinking time, a necessary hiatus since her brain seems to be addled with the drugs she takes and dragging up what she really wants to say from its anaesthetised recesses can take a long while.

Inevitably, all conversation ends up with her state of health.

'One doctor for a village this size,' she moans. 'You can never get hold of him.'

She appears to manage it more than most.

'They used to send us Bordeaux University students – from the Ivory Coast and Ghana – they were very good but that stopped when the government curbed immigration. I'm against racism, myself.'

'What do you do when you can't get hold of the doctor?'

'Try one in another village,' she says.

She's tried them all.

'If he has surgeries only three half days a week, what does the good doctor do with the rest of his time?' I'm intrigued to know.

'He's big in the Limoges Jehovah's Witnesses,' she whispers conspiratorially. 'A leader. I know they don't believe the same things we do but he's the only one who appreciates what it's like for me to be a Pentecostal here in France where no one understands. We have interesting conversations. I've told him all about you.'

I arrive home as Henri appears with a trailer full of wood and offloads it into our shed. 'A present,' he shouts genially as he drives away.

'Why a present?' I ask Peter.

'Apparently wood is worth quite a lot of money and it's his way of saying sorry for all the upheaval over the boundaries.'

'Then why doesn't he write us a blooming cheque instead? If he thinks he's getting out of his responsibilities that way . . .' but Peter has taken off and is half way across the field to take a closer look at the antics of one of our other neighbours.

Judging by the whirr of an electric cutter, Monsieur Lavale is engaged in some rather manic hedge cutting – very near our disputed boundary. It is *bornages* or boundary day tomorrow, when the court's official arbiter of boundaries will come and tell us whose is what. Monsieur Lavale appears to be preparing for the visit.

Peter is too late. The far side of our field is a mangled mess. Most of the hedgerows have been reduced to a fraction of an inch. I could cry with exasperation. It will take years for them to grow again and destroys the habitation of so much wildlife. And this is the man who is taking Henri to court for destroying *his* bushes and his trees.

Peter returns and puts an arm around my waist. 'Don't let it get to you,' he reassures me. 'It's not worth it. Once the argument is resolved and we know where the boundary is, we'll plant lots of bushes and trees.'

Wednesday, 18th October

A cold, blustery grey day dawns. The neighbours gather in a silent, sullen huddle of beige anoraks. There's Henri, Monsieur Lavale and his solicitor, the goat farmer from next door and even the Mayor, though I'm not sure why. Only the official boundary surveyor, or *géomètre*, as he's known, is in genial mood.

'Guinness, eh?' he says with a big smile, shaking Peter's hand warmly, 'My favourite.' His own name,

Gehl, sounds like *gêle*, the French word for frost, which is probably apt, given the frosty atmosphere which is the natural habitat for a man involved in resolving bitter disputes. Resentment crackles in the air already.

There are several boundaries to establish and proceedings start with a long and difficult debate on a border between Henri and Jean Lavale's farmland. Tempers soon flare. The more excited Lavale becomes, the squeakier his voice. It is irritating for everyone and Henri can barely contain himself. Peter plants himself between the two and remains detached, conciliatory.

When coffee miraculously appears over the hedge from the goat farm, Peter takes the opportunity to chat to Monsieur Gehl's assistant.

'You must find this difficult,' he suggests.

'Ah, non,' she replies, smiling, 'this is an easy one. Sometimes the solicitors have to hold the owners apart. We say nothing – in case they go for us. Oh, it can get very nasty.'

'That isn't an old map of this area you have there, is it?'

'*Bien sûr*,' she says, holding it out for him to see. 'This one dates from the time of Napoleon. It's what we use to help us form our judgement.'

'Can I see it?' Peter asks.

He takes a quick look while no one else is watching and sees straight away that the disputed trees on our boundary are ours.

'Thank you,' he says, handing the map back to her.

'You're welcome.' She smiles knowingly.

At 2pm, after five frustrating hours, it's three to Henri, one to Lavale and one to the goatfarmer. In only one of the five disputed boundaries, where Lavale was claiming an extra metre, did he have a justifiable claim. But relations, if not boundaries, are well and truly stretched. The Mayor gave up and went home for lunch at midday, before Peter could establish why he was there. He hasn't come back.

'Thank you for keeping Henri calm,' Lavale mutters to Peter, as they finally head for the boundary between our fields.

'Why don't we reach an agreement *à l'aimable*,' Peter suggests, 'informally, between friends, rather than go for the official, civic kind?'

Monsieur Gehl nods in agreement. 'That's a good idea. It's easier, quicker and cheaper.'

'I only do what my solicitor says,' stammers Lavale.

'It's for you to tell your solicitor what you want,' Monsieur Gehl counters, with obvious exasperation.

As they march on ahead of Lavale, the *géomètre* whispers to Peter, 'There is no doubt your predecessor has been a pain. But then, all these farmers are difficult. They only get involved in legal disputes because their insurance pays for it and the system is constantly being abused. Don't worry. Wait for the tribunal. You will have to pay to have your boundary staked out but it's your predecessor they all want to sue.'

When they arrive at their destination, he takes the court commission out of his pocket, studies it and mutters a low, 'Ah *non, non, non, non, non*. I cannot do this.'

After a great deal of head shaking he finally says to Peter, 'You are now the owner of this property, Monsieur Guinness, yes? Not Monsieur Bouvier?'

Peter nods.

'Then I have the wrong name here on my form, so I cannot proceed.'

'Does that matter?' Peter asks in disbelief.

'Ah, Monsieur, it is everything.'

And with that, he and his assistant pack up their belongings and take their leave, promising to come back when the court reissues the order.

'And when will that be?' Peter shouts after them.

'In a few months.'

'But I'm not here in a few months.'

Too late. Their van is already disappearing in the distance.

Henri follows us to the house. I have never seen him quite so distressed. He keeps tugging at his jaw and waving his arms and is talking so fast in local slang that we can barely understand him. The day has manifestly been an ordeal and he can't believe it isn't over yet, because this final boundary – ours – is the one that really counts. If Lavale is right that it's a metre further into our property than the current fence suggests and he sues Henri for cutting down his bushes, Henri stands to lose a great deal of money, because, he now tells us, he isn't insured.

'The problem with that man is that when there's a healthy tree on a boundary he says, "It's mine" but when the tree is dead, "It's yours. You clear it away."'

Gradually he begins to calm down. 'All the same, I'm learning from you,' he admits to Peter. 'I'm too excitable, I get so angry but you, you know how to make friends with people. I think this idea of arranging things *à l'aimable* is a very good idea.'

'Hmmmm,' I say to Peter, after he leaves. 'That will save him having to pay so much. Watch it.'

Peter reflects that though we now use the familiar *'tu'* for you, when we speak to Henri, he refuses to do the same. 'I asked him why he couldn't *tutoie* me and he said, "It wouldn't be right. You're the same age as my father." That's really cheering.'

'Nothing like a bit of respect for the elderly,' I remind him. It's a European trait we Brits could do with learning.

'Yes but not just yet, thanks.'

Thursday, 19th October

I leave Peter with the manual work and go exploring. New places, new sensations, being alone with my thoughts, has always helped me get back in touch with God on those days when I feel we're not communicating. My fault entirely, I freely admit but like any couple, we need some quality time together.

One of our nearby towns boasts a famous cathedral. I am not prepared to be impressed. When it comes to places of worship, the Jewish part of me has never been keen on Romanesque magnificence. It's monolithic, formal, cold and unfriendly compared to an intimate, brightly-painted synagogue. Even so, I am taken aback by the impact of this particular building. Amphitheatre-like and echoing though it is, the long sweep of steps leading steeply down to the altar from the porch do manage to create a sense of unworthiness, of the need to prostrate yourself before an awesome, holy God. A reminder that we can too easily become over familiar. This sense of smallness and stillness is what I need just at this moment.

On the way home, a momentary lapse of concentration jolts me cruelly out of mellow mood. I get into the wrong lane at traffic lights and end up on the wrong side of the road. Cars are coming straight at me but each one manages to swerve round me and, greater miracle, no one hoots, gives me a victory sign or gets into a rage. It must be the English car. 'These idiots – not only do they not speak our language, they want to drive on the left too!'

Behind me a queue of cars backs up one at a time, allowing me to reverse out of danger's way but not enough to see the lights. So they toot gently to let me know they have changed and an oncoming driver graciously waves me on. Oh this is so much nicer than being in England.

Except there is still no sign of the wardrobe from Atlas. But I'm not giving into furniture rage. I'm learning to chill.

Friday, 20th October

We're still not completely sure why Peter has been mandated to appear before the Tribunal in a legal wrangle that isn't ours. It's Henri who is being sued after all. Or, perish the thought, are we responsible for any damage he may have caused? Both sides now regularly call or phone to bend Peter's ear. Lavale catalogues Henri's misdeeds. He is arrogant, aggressive and destructive – the local bully. Anyone can confirm it. Henri dismisses Lavale as a retired postman, who knows nothing about farming and doesn't know how to look after his animals properly. 'He's supposed to be retired. He takes his pension and doesn't declare he is working. It's illegal. Not only that, it takes jobs from younger men and creates unemployment, *hein*?'

Early in the afternoon we hear shots very close by. For all we know it could be an old-fashioned duel – one way of solving the problem. We rush to the verandah to be treated to a display of tiny fountains appearing all over the lake.

'Someone's firing at our lake,' I announce to Peter, with a certain amount of shock.

'Jean Lavale,' he says grimly. 'It's coming from that direction.'

'What the heck is he doing?'

'I told him he could shoot coypu if he saw any on our land. Henri would never let him.'

'I'm not surprised. He seems to be firing indiscriminately. The man's a liability.'

Later, when we go down to retrieve any bodies, there are none to be found.

Peter shakes his head and laughs. 'I'll have to put a stop to it. It certainly wouldn't be much fun for any guests who go to sit by the lake for some quiet.'

On the culinary front, rural life is taking some getting used to. Though small, our local Spar has all I really need and can carry on my back and on the handle bars – but not necessarily what I want when I want it. Some days there are plums, others courgettes. Broccoli magically appears one week, never to be seen again. There's frozen spinach but no frozen peas. I'm learning to eat more simply and give thanks for whatever happens to be available.

Sunday, 22nd October

We have finally found a church. I was dreading having to make do with formal French Catholicism, liberal Protestantism, stony, evangelical Calvinism or wild Pentecostalism – which just goes to show what an exigent consumer I am. But a few days ago I had the inspiration to call in at the tourist office in Montmorillon and ask for a list of churches. A very keen assistant brought out an array of brochures offering guided tours of dozens of historic buildings but I was beyond feigning fascination after so many weeks of searching, took a deep breath and asked, '*Evangelique*?'

'Ah, oui,' she said, manifestly delighted to be able to offer this particular piece of specialist information too, took me to the window and pointed me across the square.

'Over there?' I asked. How could we have missed it all these weeks?

On the other side of the square was a narrow back street I had never noticed before. Outside a tiny glass-fronted, former shop were a stack of *Alpha News* – exactly like the English, my-life-was-a-mess-until version, only in French. 'This looks as if it might do,' I thought to myself with a real sense of excitement in the pit of my stomach and we went back today.

Around forty people, half of them French, half English, squeezed into the tiny rented building. The service couldn't be described as any denomination in particular and moved at half the normal pace, given simultaneous translation and laughter at the gaffes but the welcome was as warm as any I have ever known. They invited us to stay for lunch, along with around six other visitors who had brought no contribution either but it seems they're used to that, as food just kept on coming. I sat next to Marinette, who founded the church with her farmer husband, and that was a very good place to sit. Her *rôti de boeuf* and *tarte tatin* were to die for. But apart from that, we talked without drawing breath for around an hour, as only two women who know instinctively that they're soul sisters can.

Marinette is very un-farmer's wife, in chic chiffon and with well-cut, pretty silver curls. She told me that, six years ago, she and her husband Patrick and two other couples, all members of the Baptist Church in Poitiers, some forty minutes away, decided to form a local home group. It grew and reluctantly, as they loved their church and didn't relish looking after spiritual sheep on top of a seventy-hour farming week, they felt they had no alternative but to metamorphose into a church. It is the first and only Protestant church for four hundred years in an area of around ten thousand people. Next weekend a South American ex-gangster is coming to preach. And I thought that coming to France for a sabbatical might be a rather dull alternative to visiting churches across the globe.

It is a glorious late afternoon, warm and balmy, with the trees a wonderful array of green and gold, ochre and crimson. Peter and I take our Sabbath jaunt by bike again. I thought we were energetic until I see dozens of elderly French men and matrons, miles from the nearest village, diving under trees, leaping into ditches, grovelling under bushes. It's mushroom season and they're after buried treasure – *cêpes* and *truffes*. Henri is convinced that we have a plentiful supply in our garden and I would love to tell the hordes to pop round and that they are welcome to them. I can't quite bring myself to try them. Just my luck they'd turn out to be toadstools. The French equivalent of DEFRA issues a free colour DVD every year to anyone wanting to distinguish between the deadly and the genuine article. Every pharmacist is also a trained fungi analyst and will advise on samples taken to them. Even so, last week two people ended up in Tours Hospital having liver transplants after eating what they thought were wild mushrooms. We may have a garden full of delicacies but I'm buying mine from the supermarket. Ah, we townies, we would starve rather than take any chances.

We met a professional gardener at the church this morning, thank you God – an Englishman called Jon. We badly need his advice about what to grow where. The particular field venerated by Henri's cows is a quagmire. Local maps all show a stream running through its middle, flowing into the bottom of our lake. It has mysteriously disappeared. Henri says Lavale has deliberately deflected it at source to dry up the lake. Lavale claims it was Henri who blocked it to flood his fields, despite the fact that it's our field that's flooded. Whatever, we will have to re-establish it if the field is to be of any use.

Monday, 23rd October

The first real autumnal nip in the air is the signal for the French to begin a manic building of log piles for their winter fires. Every house has a growing mountain of wood bricks outside, chopped with precision and care. Every house owner knows exactly how many bricks are in each pile, what year they were chopped in, what quality they are and when they will be ready to burn. Wealth is measured in wood. People are described as, 'wood rich.' We have had so many questions about whether we have collected enough wood yet that Peter is panic chopping. He has rushed out into the garden and begun hacking our fallen oak into pieces, taking them by wheelbarrow to the shed and stacking them in neat piles in date order – even though we're not likely to be here in the winter for at least eight years. Maybe it's the caveman instinct to store and gather – to keep us cosy. Sweet.

When he isn't chopping, he's mowing. Bought to cut swathes through long grass, which ours will inevitably become, the new mower is so powerful that it reminds me of a large, disobedient dog taking its master for a walk. Pulled-through-a-hedge-backwards has never seemed so apposite an adjective to describe my husband these days – especially given the need and fear to employ the services of a French barber.

Tuesday, 24th October

Physical work is restorative. Peter has an energy and vitality I haven't seen in him for a very long time and if this sabbatical can do no more than that, it will have achieved a great deal.

Church ministry has never been tougher. Ministers have been in the thick of one of the greatest social upheavals of all time, when Sunday trading, mistrust of institutions, post-modern individualism and a break-down in traditional morality have driven a rail road through church communities, demolishing some com-pletely. And ministers are often held responsible for the fall-out. Most have largely survived the dereliction alone. It reminds me of a wonderful Dave Allen sketch, from the days when kids played at domino rallies. The priest leans on the back pew of his empty church, which collapses and sets up a crumbling domino effect that runs round the whole church.

Not only that but there's the raft of new legislation that requires paperwork in triplicate – health and safety, the Charities Act, child protection, fire regulations and employment law. It's enough to turn any minister into a glorified bureaucrat, that is if they survive the threats, harassment and potential assault on their own doorstep.

In the thick of it with him, like standing in fog, I couldn't see just how utterly exhausted he had become. Rescue has come just in time.

It's so good to feel physically tired at the end of a day.

'Isn't the silence wonderful after living over the A6?' I whisper to him as we settle down for the night. We have had to put up with the roar of lorries hurtling past our vicarage window for the past fifteen years.

'It would be without the constant whirr from the goat cheese farm down the road,' he says.

'What whirr?' I'm disconcerted. It's the tranquillity I value more than anything else. I get up, go to the door, stand and listen. Silence. It's only Peter's tinnitus and I go back to bed happy.

Wednesday, 25th October

Ay, me, we have yet another legal battle on our hands. This time it's the boundary between the far side of the lake and the little wood behind it. No wonder Henri was reluctant to help us buy the wood when we bought the house. The Delgras family, to whom it has belonged for generations, have apparently accused him of felling some of their trees and of stealing three measures of wood from their land. They intend to sue him but first they have to prove that what he took was theirs and not his. And that, oh yes, means having the legal boundary established.

The little wood is actually a long-neglected mess, its paths blocked by fallen trees and overgrown with brambles and briers. Henri says he would love to *nettoye* (clean) it, which is a funny word to use about woodland but he wouldn't dare, because that's what he was doing when he was accused of stealing. Stealing, he exclaims, in disgust, as if! Why should he take three measly measures of the Delgras's wood when he owns most of the woodland between here and the village?

'That's a very good point,' I say to Peter after he has gone. A hothead, yes, rude, yes, unthinking, I have no doubt he can be all of those but I can't see him as dishonest. Why would he want to take a pile of wood? Or am I naive? After all, he never told us about the legal battles when we bought the house.

Thursday, 26th October

The couple who run the goat's cheese farm down the road, answer, like a pair of puppets, to the names of Patrice and Patricia. This has become a very happy relationship since we first met them on boundary day. We popped in to say hello and now Patricia arrives regularly, not just with any old goat's cheese but with a variety of her special concoctions – rolled in chopped shallots or smothered in spices or, best of all, filled with redcurrant jam, a bit like a jam doughnut. I am trying hard to think what English delicacy I can take her in return but nothing comes easily to mind. A crumble? There's no fruit to be had to put in it. Apples are very plentiful but not the tart Bramleys that make a crumble so special. Flapjack might be a possibility if I could find golden syrup. Patricia tells me her youngest son is training to be a pastry chef. He is apprenticed to a master and it will be several years before he is fully qualified. Patisserie is still an art in France. There are no short-cuts, no ready-made pastry cases, choux buns or meringue baskets. He makes every part of the confection – eclairs, *tartes*, chocolate *truffles*, almond biscuits. I'm rethinking the flapjack.

The goat farm is only the most recent in a long line of businesses that Patrice seems to follow at whim and change every six years since the time he decided that being an electrician was far too dull. Every time they move, Patricia makes it her business to find something that will integrate her quickly into village life and help her to understand its local customs. Patrice is a reserved man, happy with his goats but for her, selling goat's cheese in the village square on Saturday mornings has been a lifeline. Some customers chat all day. There is nothing and no one she doesn't know. She is a mine of useful information. And little that we do that escapes her notice either.

It is obvious she doesn't like or trust Henri. 'That family – the Bouviers – they have a reputation around these parts.'

I raise my eyebrows.

'A bit – what shall I say?' she explains, turning her palms up and down, willing me to understand.

'Not . . . Mafioso,' I try, in a hushed voice.

She laughs.

'You said it. Everyone is a little afraid of them. The papa is known to be a bit . . . maybe threatening. So yes, I'm not surprised Henri has left you with a number of issues. He's a bit lax in matters financial.'

This is a real disappointment. She sees it but reassures us that the Delgras are a pleasant old pair, who will be very amenable to resolving any issues with us in the nicest possible way. They own a ramshackle old family house opposite the goat farm but it is empty most of the time because they live elsewhere. But, Patricia says, they'll almost certainly be there at the end of the month. They never miss the big local farmers' market.

As we set off on the thirty-mile trip for our first church home group, which doesn't begin until 8.30 in the evening, to give its members time for a tranquil evening meal, I remind Peter of Patricia's warning. At night wild animals leap out from the forests into the path of unsuspecting motorists. Only a fortnight ago a deer crashed into the side of her car and did some serious damage. She was lucky. It might have been a wild boar. It occurs to me it must be galling for her husband, President of the local hunt, to spend a weekend looking for the creatures – often in vain – only to have one land on his car during the week.

I love passing through the tiny clusters of houses built outside the villages for small farming communities. These hamlets have the strangest names, such as The Age, The Slippers, The Brushes – imagine telling the English you live 'over at The Brushes.' Perhaps the names are a recognition of the fact that most of the inhabitants are well into decrepitude. It is a salutary reminder that we are here to see whether we could face a more permanent uprooting and replanting in retirement – a mere eight years hence. There is a sense in which being cut off from all I have known and from all who know me, has been an interesting time of dislocation. At first I couldn't bear the loss of the familiar, of purpose, direction, busyness and structure and couldn't wait to go home. But gradually, the slow pace of life here, the gentle daily routine of work, study and play, the tranquil nights have been working a kind of magic and I am beginning to feel that this could enable a meaningful slide into old age one day.

There is no doubt there would be work to do in the tiny, struggling French church that cannot afford a full-time minister and is hungry to be pastored and taught. There are about ten of us gathered at the home of Barry and Jean, having travelled around three hundred miles between us. Barry and Jean, a retired English couple, were members of the Salvation Army at home. Barry leads the home group in English, with various attempts by the French at simultaneous translation when we remember they are there. I marvel at the welcome extended by the indigenous French to their English incomers, translating everything, graciously putting up with long extempore English prayers that even the English find hard to follow. One or two of my countrymen, I'm told tonight, accept the generous, French welcome at the beginning then, as they do in England, drop out when church doesn't meet their expectations and they can't be bothered to go any more because, after all, 'Sunday is our only day for us.' They are retired, for goodness sake! At least there is no alternative congregation where they can go through the process again. The English that do stick with the French church, like Barry and Jean, and generously give their time and hospitality, even if they can't do it in French, are a great encouragement. There is no doubt about that.

Marinette delivers a bolt from the blue. She has had a call from the estate agents to say the family who rent out the little shop that serves as a church want to sell it. The congregation has the first chance to buy – at a grossly inflated price – but if they don't want to, they must vacate the building by the end of the month. This is difficult. The shop is right in the centre of town and the higher profile provided by a shop window prevents them being seen as a sect. Before the authorities allowed them a licence at all, they had to prove they were a bona fide church by demonstrating their affiliation to an accepted denomination. Since the congregation consists of a motley of Baptists, Mennonites, Pentecostals, Salvationists and Anglicans, each preferring allegiance to their own denomination – apart from the Anglicans of course – this was a source of some disagreement and threatened the church's very existence from the start. They began with the Mennonites, strong in Alsace Lorraine, Patrick's home territory. But Herique, one of the leaders, works for the army and his brother-in-law,

Daniel, is a policeman and neither felt comfortable with Mennonite pacifism. There were inadequacies in every denominational statement of belief, so now they have their own hotch-potch conditions of membership.

'The shop is very public and that's good for our relations in the town,' says Herique, a slim, gracious, bespectacled man, with a winning smile.

'But on the other hand, it is becoming too small,' sighs Marinette. 'We have been here before,' she admits, 'many times. We will just wait and see – like we always do. We renovated it and painted it but if we have to move, so be it. God will find us somewhere else.'

It all sounds a bit *Fiddler on the Roof* – the experience of my ancestors in Eastern Europe, hanging loose to bricks and mortar, ready to pack up and move at a moment's notice. Being church in France is manifestly not straightforward.

What with two languages, large slices of Marinette's cinnamon and apple cake and endless rounds of kissing on departure, we don't get home until well after midnight – fortunately without meeting the local wild life.

Friday, 27th October

I am very struck by the story of Nehemiah. At a time when the exiles return to Jerusalem, Nehemiah is cupbearer to the King of Babylon. He has status, creature comforts and financial security and ostensibly throws it all away to join a rag-taggle band of immigrants in rebuilding the wall – and that against fierce opposition.

Perhaps giving up my NHS career was not momentary madness after all. There is other work to be done, walls for me to build – but whether here or at home, I can't yet say. What if we came out here without a pension with a view to supporting the beleaguered little band that is the French church? Would that be foolhardy or are we being tested on our willingness to live more simply, to take the risks that are so contrary to our nature and the norm in our society?

Need does not constitute call, I've heard that so often. On the other hand, hard on the heels of Nehemiah's story is Esther's. This time it's the Queen of Babylon who risks her very life for the sake of her people. She responds to the need. These Old Testament stories can be very unsettling.

I call on Marguerite to tell her we have found a church. The doorbell plays *Gentille Alouette*, inducing an instant, totally unexpected, lump-in-the-throat blast from my past. I haven't heard that children's song about stroking a gentle dove since my dad sang it to me when I was very little. '*Je te plumerai la tête*' – I used to repeat it after him, pointing to my head, then, '*et le nez*', pointing to my nose and '*et la bouche*', pointing to my mouth. Perhaps that was the start of my love affair with France.

Marguerite, though still in the dressing gown, looks positively cheerful. Bruno's thirty-five-year-old has taken flight, she tells me before I'm barely through the door. She has her revenge. God is answering her prayers. The news about the church pales by comparison. She says there's a chance Bruno might come to church with her now. From what I have heard I think that's about as likely as a bull staying celibate in a field of heifers but I'm not going to spoil her moment of glory. We'll pick her up on Sunday.

Back at home, Peter is checking the house insurance policy to see whether it includes boundary disputes. Every possible dispute with neighbours is covered, all legal advice is paid for in every circumstance, except, in block capitals, ARGUMENTS OVER BOUNDARIES. Manifestly, we are not the first to find ourselves in this situation. A clergy stipend won't go very far in France.

Studying the policy, we notice under 'Principle Definitions' that 'others' refers to any victim of damages, except 'you, your *conjoint*, or your *concubin*.' Concubine? He should be so lucky! Partners are simply 'conjoints' in French law then. Anything else is a concubine.

'I promise you your wardrobe will be here next week, Madame,' Atlas reassures me.

Saturday, 28th October

We pass the Delgras house when we're out walking. The front door is open and an elderly man is installing a thick, ugly green fly screen that will block out their only daylight. But the French don't seem to mind. They keep their shutters shut. They like living in the dark.

'Hello,' we call, 'we're your new neighbours.'

'Ah,' he says genially, coming over to us at once, his hand held out. 'We've been waiting to meet you.'

He's a dear old man with rosy cheeks, a small white moustache and a twinkle in his eye.

'Jeanne,' he calls out, beckoning us to follow him into the house, 'Jeanne, our new neighbours have come to pay us a visit.'

A stout, smiling old woman in a pinny, leaning heavily on a stick, comes towards us as fast as her disability will allow and, ignoring our protests, ushers us in.

The Delgras live in a traditional *longère*. There is no hallway, only three rooms, each leading off the other. We pass through a storeroom stacked to the ceiling with shelves of jams and pickles and their bedroom to get to the sitting room, where there are no armchairs. In typical French fashion we sit around the table. All social interaction, even watching TV takes place around the table. I'd noticed that at Marguerite's. In the corner is an old, lace-covered double bed.

'Traditional Limousin,' Jeanne says, following my quizzical gaze. 'My ancestors ate, slept and lived in the one room. We don't use the bed – unless we have visitors, nieces or nephews and then it's handy.'

Apparently, many French still live in just one room. In farming communities spare downstairs rooms are for the animals. The entire upstairs of a house is purely a barn for storing grain and animal fodder. No wonder that restoring these houses, the great English pastime, can be a nightmare.

'I hope you don't mind the way we English are buying up France,' I say apologetically.

They laugh. 'If it were not for the English, much of France would now be in ruins,' Jeanne says. 'Have you seen our local *chateau*? English people are restoring it at last. It used to belong to minor aristocrats but their son sold his soul to Lucifer. A statue of Satan was found in his bed. Needless to say, the family line ended.'

Jeanne excuses herself and makes a phone call.

'Come quickly,' she says, 'the new English neighbours are here.'

'Roland and Anne,' she explains, 'my nephew and his partner. Once this legal battle is resolved I'm going to give them the little wood across the lake. You must meet them.'

She takes four rather cloudy-looking champagne glasses out a large, heavy oak sideboard, polishes them on her pinny, then fetches a bottle from her store. 'Sour cherries preserved in eau de vive,' she announces proudly, squinting at the label. '2003.'

'One of Jeanne's little delicacies,' says Albert, her husband, with a wink. 'Eat the cherries first – and then
drink the liqueur – slowly. It will warm every part of
you.'

We spit the stones into a dish in the middle of the
table. That and the pure alcohol, flavoured with cherry
juice, certainly helps to break the ice.

The Delgras recount the slow and obviously painful
story of how their son died of Multiple Sclerosis three
years ago. He was 43 and their only child. They show no
trace of bitterness, never ask the inevitable. 'Why?' But
describe with tears in their eyes the long, nursing
process and how wonderful their brave, uncomplaining
Michel was.

'And now all I have left are my three nephews,' says
Jeanne, wiping her eyes on a large checked handkerchief. 'They're good to me, especially Roland, who has
the house at the bottom of the village.'

Roland is a tall middle-aged man with such a large
handle-bar moustache that it's hard to make out what
he's saying. When he speaks, it sounds as if he's gargling. He and his partner, a dainty, diminutive little
woman with a bob, greet us warmly – despite our
groans when he tells us they work for France Telecom.
Ah, they laugh, it's all Orange's fault. Things have never
been the same since the takeover. And now France
Telecom is buying up England too, starting with BT, so
there's no escape – not even for the English. In fact, it's
probably revenge for their invasion of France – a very
sophisticated and contemporary version of war. If you
take over our country, we have a more subtle means of
taking over yours.

Roland and Anne only come to the commune at week-
ends but plan to move here permanently and farm as
soon as it's financially feasible to ditch their day jobs.

Commuting on the TGV from Tours to Paris four days a week is becoming unbearable, not to mention the standards of working life when they get there.

The four assure us that they want to have good relations with us. And we, in our turn, say that we will respect their land. Jeanne tells us that it has been in her family for generations and never, in all that time – and her memory seems to go back to mediaeval days – has anyone had to deal with a villain like Henri.

'Michel never liked or trusted him,' she informs us. And there is no answer to that.

Sunday, 29th October

Bruno, a big, rough-looking man, is waiting for Marguerite when we drop her back home after church. He's pacing the floor ready for his dinner and it reduces Marguerite to a dithering, apologetic bundle of nerves.

'This is the little English woman I told you about, my new friend,' she explains, as I help her out of the car.

Bruno pushes his cap back, scratches his head loudly, grunts and extends a grudging hand. He has something in his mouth revolving visibly around his tongue, like a piece of laundry in a washing machine. Marguerite's introduction is greeted with no sign of diminished grumpiness and we take our leave quickly.

'Did you say a thirty-five-year-old went off with him?' Peter asks incredulously, as we turn into our drive. 'Do women go for that?'

'Don't go there, my darling,' I say. 'Not if you want to enjoy your Sunday lunch. And anyway, she's just left him. There's a surprise.'

Barry has lent me Philip Yancey's *Disappointment with God*. It's an apposite time for it, as in my daily readings I have reached the story of poor old Job. I'm a spiritual sumo wrestler. I envy childlike acceptance but it's not my natural state. I'm constantly in God's face with a raft of questions and complaints, mainly about why he can appear to intervene in the little things, yet is missing in the mind-blowingly big and painful. Why guide us so clearly to the house here and not heal a dear friend of cancer? 'If you'd been here my brother, Lazarus, wouldn't have died,' the feisty Martha flings at Jesus. Too right but there was a reason for his absence – a higher purpose. As there must always be. I just wish I could live with mystery with more equanimity.

Does prayer make any difference? When am I using God as my servant, expecting him to dance to my tune, rather than my dancing to the music of heaven? After all, I don't have his perspective. And even when I do get one amazing answer – like this house – it will be a mere few hours before I want another and still doubt it will ever happen. Yancey says that even God's constant, almost physical, presence in the wilderness, his actual voice, his miracles galore, didn't make the Children of Israel any more believing. If anything, the more he intervened in their lives, the more faithless and disobedient they became.

I wonder whether hearing God isn't a bit like satellite navigation – silent when we're going in the right direction, only prompting when we need it. 'Turn right, turn left, turn around when possible.'

And maybe the reason I can't fully trust is that I'm one of those people who can't quite believe that when things are going well, something won't go wrong. It's a recording in my head – a voice from childhood. My mother and her fatalism. Job would never have known loss if he hadn't enjoyed what he had. Would I still hold on if I lost everything? How can we ever really know? Job had no means of knowing what was coming. And just as well. Sitting here in the comfort of my own home at last, it's easy to forget how fragile we are. I just hope that in the event of such loss, that I would be given a Job kind of 'survival' faith – earthy and bloody-minded as it was.

October 30th

We may well have landed in a *trou perdu* – in the middle of nowhere – but, we discover that once a month a tiny village just ten minutes to the north of us plays host to one of the biggest *foires* or farmers' markets in France. A local sign tells the world it's on the 29th of every month. It does not say that this month it's on the 30th, because it moves to a Monday if the 29th happens to be a Sunday. Local knowledge is all.

'Don't go in July or August,' says Marguerite, 'all the tourists are there. Don't go in March or April either – everyone's buying new livestock. And I wouldn't go in December – the fight for poultry!'

'Any other month is safe?'

'Well I wouldn't bother with November or February either – half term.'

The Delgras have told us we must go. Everyone does – to see and be seen.

'One *restauranteur* orders 160 kilograms of calves' heads just for the occasion,' Jeanne said with excitement.

The *foire*, apparently, is the only place where you can sit down to a decent calf's head stew these days. 'Be there by 8am,' Albert warns us, 'or you'll queue.'

It's our sabbatical and we only do leisurely, so arrive at 9.30 am and find that Albert is right. Our tiny village, which never normally has any through traffic, has become a major thoroughfare. We travel in convoy through tiny country roads, then queue for around twenty minutes to pay our one euro parking fee, treated all the while to the sight of the rural masses in too short trousers marching with baskets full of produce, boxes that wriggle and make strange sounds or handfuls of squawking chickens swung from their legs.

The *foire* is an extraordinary mixture of the mundane and the bizarre, exploitative Blackpool-style *schloch* and fascinating knick-knacks. The smell from vast joints of dried wild boar and hams, bathtub sized cheeses and stalls full of nothing but garlic leaves one feeling a little queasy at this time of day, not to mention the platefuls of snails in oil, frog legs in aspic and, to our astonishment, coypu paté, called euphemistically, '*paté de lapin des lacs*' – lake rabbit paté. It fetches a grand price.

'We could be making a fortune,' I say to Peter, 'if you could catch them and I had the stomach to skin and fillet them.' We have heard that people return from a sabbatical ready for a new direction in life but on reflection, this probably isn't it.

We take our leave with a tray of tomatoes and a pair of one euro knickers and head instead for the glories of La Brenne, the nature park and bird sanctuary just to the north of us. We marvel, as we drive slowly through breathtakingly beautiful country lanes, that we have been given the luxury of the time to enjoy such a paradise.

'I feel alive again,' Peter says, as we revel in the green and golds, the gentle streams and quaint old farmhouses. It seems strange to realise that we weren't before and didn't even know it – that's what's so shocking. The other evening, as we finished a game of Scrabble, glee-fully beating our highest overall score so far, I said to him, 'Why do we never play Scrabble at home?' 'It wouldn't cross our minds,' he said, 'not with all the important things there are to do instead.'

Or have we simply lost touch with what is important, consumed with doing, not being?

We have to admit there is no permanent escape from stress – not even here. The conflicting stories that sur-round the battle over our boundaries have thoroughly confused us. We no longer know whom to believe.

'Marguerite can't understand why no one likes our predecessors,' I reflect to Peter, as we take a stroll.

She now regularly demands that her 'pastor's wife' calls for tea and sympathy. I comply, though I never play the part at home. Funny to find myself doing it here.

'She says Henri and Madeleine are the only ones in the commune who are nice to her. I asked her why she thought they were so disliked. She told me it was "You have one more sheep than me" nonsense.' Jealousy, amongst grown men, I asked her? Yes, she said, that was all it was.

But maybe jealousy is only half the story. Isn't it possible that with his temper and precipitous actions, Henri has brought local antagonism down on himself? Lavale claims that he destroyed his own bushes, hedgerows, trees, fenc-ing and walls in various fits of pique. We have been sad-dened at the number of stories we are hearing about French farmers with scant regard for environmental issues, who wilfully fell beautiful old trees and destroy hedgerows. There are, Peter has discovered, several self-indulgent rea-sons for what is becoming the wholesale deforestation of France. Government tax concessions and bigger European Community subsidies are based on acreage. Both Lavale and Henri have told him that land is measured by satellite.

'They think they're being watched continually by unseen forces. Henri warned me in dead earnest, "Don't try to reforest your land too quickly," and then, pointing upwards said "*They* don't like it." Big Brother, eh?'

'They're freaked by Google Earth,' Peter laughs. 'Someone is up there taking those photographs. It makes them paranoid.'

The upshot is, they think that clear land means larger acreage, so cut down trees and hedgerows to get more money.

'So is that the real reason Henri removed trees and bushes? Or was it Lavale, as Henri claims, who is trying to make a little extra? The problem is, I think they're both capable of it.'

'I'm sure they are,' Peter agrees.

The prophets Isaiah, Jeremiah and Ezekiel, upon whose dire warnings I will soon embark, were clear that the love of money and the greed it induced was at the heart of all injustice, violence, oppression and exploitation. Their voices from several thousand years ago are strangely contemporary. Human beings never change – and rarely learn the lessons of history.

I tell him that Jon, our gardener friend from the church, has explained to me that another reason the locals play fast and loose with their land is that the government has made it clear that burning wood is one of the most viable, renewable sources of energy. So they use it for cheap fuel in the winter. 'Nobody seems to have told them that the energy is only renewable if you plant as many trees as you cut down. That's far too sensible.'

'And too much work. And then,' Peter adds, from hard and heartfelt experience with our new mower, 'it is so much easier, so much less time-consuming, if a tractor can work in a field devoid of obstacles.'

Jon has also told us that one of his neighbours recently dispensed with twenty magnificent, ancient oaks. When Jon asked him why, he simply said, 'Because they're mine and who's going to stop me?' I felt like going over and stuffing Walter Breuggeman's theology of the land down his smug little gullet. 'Ah, *non, Monsieur le fermier*, the trees are not yours to murder as you please. They have a life of their own. They could have given pleasure to your grandchildren and great-grandchildren. They could have been here long after you are manure.'

I reflect on how often, even at home, a tree can simply be an object that gets in the way – usually of parking the car – rather than a symbol of the continuity of creation and the faithfulness of its Creator.

When we call in on Patricia, the goat farmer's wife, she tells us that she suspects that part of our lake may actually belong to Albert and Jeanne. The courts may insist that we drain or buy it. How she knows this, we're not sure. But she has her sources.

'But we can share it,' we tell her, magnanimously. 'We don't mind who enjoys our land.'

'*Attention*,' she replies, wagging her finger, 'Local people are very attached to the land they inherit from their parents and very possessive with their half metres. You may welcome them but they will never show you the same courtesy.'

Tuesday, 31st October

A huge change of temperature today. Suddenly it's high summer again, with a low sun and long shadows, the thermometer reading 24 degrees. Does the weather know what month it is?

Peter has taken himself out into the garden to dig a trench that will drain our waterlogged field. It's back-breaking work but my incorrigible trench-digger loves it. This is the man who used to take a garden spade to the beach when the children were little, so that he could create streams in the sand.

'Have you seen that idiot over there?' my dad was once asked by a passer by, as he sat on a bench watching.

'Yes I have. That idiot's my son-in-law.'

I watch a lone figure, digging and shovelling happily, oblivious of the twenty years that have passed. In my daily readings I have reached the Psalms and when he crawls into the house some four hours later, groaning, tell him that Psalm 7 is very appropriate – 'He who digs a hole and scoops it out, falls into the pit he has made.'

'Hmmph,' he says, unamused. 'Maybe that's more relevant for our neighbour.'

He has found huge trenches just over the fence and is convinced it was Lavale who deflected the stream and ruined our field.

I tell him I've also been reading, 'Lead me in a straight path because of my enemies' and think it means living openly, honestly and with as much integrity as we can muster. Peter leaves a message on Lavale's answer machine, inviting him for coffee and a chance to resolve the issue of the blocked source of the stream. Ominously, there has been no reply. Lavale, we remember, does nothing without consulting his solicitor.

Peter says Albert stopped by for a chat when he saw him working in the field and warned him that Lavale may not be very accommodating. He has known him all his life and he's very much a glass-half-empty man – always worrying about things that may never happen.

Peter apologised that he had inadvertently cut the grass on the other side of the pond, not realising that it might not belong to him.

'Oh *zut, alors,*' said Albert, clamping his hand to his head in a gesture of mock horror. He told Peter not to worry. There is no question of asking the tribunal to have the lake drained. If it is partly on their land we will simply share it amicably. We like Albert more and more and cannot believe him capable of any animosity. Losing their only son, having no immediate descendant to inherit their land has fine-tuned their sense of what is important.

While Peter was out Marguerite calls in floods of tears. Tomorrow is All Saints' Day – Toussaint – when the French lay chrysanthemums on the graves of their loved ones. She had bought a huge bunch for the grave of her grandson, a haemophiliac, who died of AIDS at the age of eighteen after being given contaminated blood.

She gave the chrysanths to Bruno to look after, since he was taking her to the grave but he left them in her garage and she's only just found them. They're dead and she has no money for any more. Why does he treat her like this? She sobs. I don't know how to respond. I can hardly say, 'I'm not surprised. Your ex is a slob, Madame.' Even if it is the truth.

Marguerite is calmer when I bring her to the door, with an '*Oh Susanna*' on the bell. Company is what she really needs. She regales me with angry tales – not so much about Bruno as about her naughty landlord: our neighbour, Lavale. She tells me how a few weeks ago she became aware of a terrible smell and hordes of flies emanating from the shed next to her garage. It was so bad that even the postman knocked on her door to ask her what the stink was. Her physiotherapist ran in with a handkerchief clamped to her nose.

'I went to investigate,' she whispers, leaning close to me, with a glance over her shoulder, 'and found the shed full of dead sheep carcasses.'

There's a pause to let me absorb this information.

'You see what I have to contend with?' she slaps the table, triumphantly, 'He leaves his dead sheep for days, stinking out the whole neighbourhood and causing all these horrible fly infestations. Then he sends his men in the middle of the night to take them away, so no one can see how many have died – because he doesn't look after them.'

She phoned the agent and asked him to tell Lavale she wasn't prepared to stand for it and Lavale arrived on her doorstep in minutes, in an absolute fury that a mere tenant had grassed him up. By then she had washed all the outside and inside walls with *eau de javel* – a very strong bleach that's used as a cure-all in most European countries.

'I can't stand that smell,' he whined.

A Jewish woman would have retorted, 'What do you want me to use, Chanel Number 5?' but she actually said, 'It's a darn sight better than the stink of your dead sheep.'

For a while there were no more carcasses but now, she says, he has started his tricks all over again. I report our conversation back to Peter as evidence that Lavale is as neglectful and egotistical as Henri says he is. 'Yes but let's be sensible,' Peter replies. 'Sheep die – and the best time to clear them away is in coolest part of the day.'

Smoke and mirrors, I really can't get to the bottom of who is telling the truth. Is there anywhere like this commune for conflicting rumours and tales?

November

'The boundary lines have fallen for me in pleasant places,' says my Psalm this morning. 'My inheritance is a good 'un.' It is indeed, plus or minus a few vital centimetres.

I cycle into the village for my usual daily bread and find the square is heaving, packed with people in black standing around looking uncomfortable. They have all been to Mass, a rare occurrence in our village church. The local *curé* has eighteen churches in his care – at the last count – and rarely finds his way here. He used to have some help from an old retired priest, the epitome of what the role once was – a round jolly toby-jug of a man, who kept a housekeeper, liked his food and drink and used to parade through the village wearing a long, black cassock and wide-brimmed hat. He conducted Mass in the village every Sunday. Marguerite went once to see what it was like and found herself the only one there. He insisted on going through the motions with her all the same. She didn't stop him as she thought it would be rude but even she had to admit that there was a strange irony in his saying Mass for one lone Pentecostal.

There is no bread to be had. Everyone is providing lunch for out-of-town family and friends. On All Saints Day people do a kind of grave tour and may visit as many as five or six different cemeteries in one area, depending on where their relatives are taking their eternal rest. It reminds me of the days between the Jewish New Year and the Day of Atonement, when Jews travel miles to visit the graves of loved ones, except that they have a whole week in which to do it, not just one day. It is a good annual tradition, a communal sharing in the grief and bereavement that never completely goes away.

I wish someone had warned me. There is no bread to be had anywhere. Amelie, the baker's wife is very pregnant and has swollen feet. She is never open on Wednesdays anyway, since government legislation of a one day a week closure cannot be overruled even for a *fête*. And the Spar has run out.

For today's little sight-seeing trip, Peter and I decide to join the cemetery crawl. The graves are a riot of colour, covered in flowers – roses and lilies, as well as chrysanthemums. Some display photographs of the deceased. Some are decorated with paintings of favourite places or children's drawings and tributes. The gravestones are all different shapes and sizes and colours. And they say things like 'In memory of my beloved Uncle Jacquot', or 'My dear friend, Marie', or 'My darling Daddy.' Clearly there is no 'acceptable' code of wording or English decorum for gravestones here. In France, they can put 'Dad' or 'Mum' on the tombstone or slip into slang if they want.

The Jews put stones, not flowers on graves. Stones cannot wither and fade, any more than memories of loved ones or their bequest. Stones are symbols of eternal love and existence. Yet these French graves, so lovingly festooned in flowers, though the interred may have been mourned and missed for many years, tell me that every member of the community is valued, whatever their age or status.

Thursday, 2nd November

I seem to have got myself onto Marks and Spencer's emailing system, probably because I was daft enough to contact customer services and complain that their shops never stocked clothes my size. There's a limit to how long middle-aged minnows can go on haunting the children's departments. I never got a reply – just pictures of Per Una's mouthwatering winter collection, which are now causing me huge shopping withdrawal symptoms.

I brought three pairs of trousers, two skirts and a dress with me for the whole three months and thought it should be enough for any woman. To be honest, when I was deciding what I would need, I felt ashamed of my bulging wardrobe and decided to take the opportunity to try and live a little more simply. Friends who know me would laugh. In fact, I do only need the basics and didn't miss what I hadn't got – until I caught sight of those website pictures, when my perfectly adequate collection suddenly seemed so featureless and boring. Heavens, I'm like a recovering alcoholic. I just have to see pictures of clothes again and I'm salivating. What temptations consumerism spreads before us. The eyes certainly have it. Didn't Jesus say something about plucking them out if they lead us astray? Perhaps I should cast my computer into the lake. Radical action is needed if I'm to be satisfied with the fulfilment of my needs and not my imagined wants, that cloy when I get them in my hands.

On the other hand, I've just read that the Proverbial good wife is 'clothed in linen and purple', oh and in 'strength and dignity.' It's all very well being here for three months. As a dedicated townie I can say, 'I'll be home in time for the winter sales.' But what if we really did live here – with no shops for miles around? Could I learn to work on the strength and dignity and forget the fine linen?

I don't think I really believed the dire warnings about wild beasts roaming the roads at night – despite Marinette attending the funeral of one of the teachers at her daughter's school, whose car had left the road and upended in a ditch when an owl collided with her windscreen. But tonight, on the way to home group, a huge, black mass ambled in front of us across the road. It was a massive wild boar, as solid as a tank.

I couldn't help but notice (oh, the distractions from prayer and serious study), that Marinette wears some very natty outfits – decent jeans, interesting bling and tonight a purple leather jacket. There must be *haute couture* out there somewhere. Should I ask where? I succumb. She tells me she goes to Poitiers – over an hour away.

Still no sign of the Atlas wardrobe. They are really sorry but with Toussaint and the statutory week's holiday, everything is late. Maybe this is a message from above saying that being without a wardrobe is good for my soul.

Friday, 3rd November

Our sleep is being disturbed by constant nightmares. Can it be explained by the intense darkness of a shuttered bedroom, so that we can't tell night from day? Or the profound, almost heavy silence after years of sleeping over a lorry highway? Could it be deep, niggling doubts about the wisdom of spending all our savings on this one purchase? Or the coming to terms with the realisation that this place will be the scene for the rest of the rest of our lives and our next home will be of the eternal variety? We're not sure. What we do know is that this current lifestyle is obviously such an unusual state of affairs that the subconscious simply won't let us rest in peace and reminds us regularly that we will soon enough be thrown back into the whirlpool of demand and busyness that constitutes our normal life in England. Peter keeps dreaming that he is speaking at a large church conference and has left his briefcase with his notes in it at the conference centre reception. He goes to his bedroom, only to discover it has been allocated to someone else. He returns to reception to discover they haven't another room, or his briefcase and his notes. Then he remembers his diary is in the briefcase too and he has no idea what he should be doing next.

He dreams the same dream over and over again, night after night. It seems to be work-related – a reflection of the barrage of pressure that is inevitable in leading any large organisation, the inability to get on top of it, the sense of inadequacy it engenders and the uncertainty about the future – both his and the church's. He is aware that after fifteen years in the same job he urgently needs new vision.

My dreams involve constantly taking wrong turnings and getting lost – a product, I suspect, of having given up a demanding full-time job and facing the fear that I don't know what to do next. Or whether there will be any next – and I'll be sent away by church and state, like Florence Nightingale, to crochet in my drawing room.

There is no doubt that stress has been our predominant companion for many years. We both lost pleasure in life and peace of mind, probably a long time ago, had we but realised it. In my daily readings the prophet Isaiah chides the people of Israel for chasing after idols. I am forcefully confronted by Philip Yancey's proposition that the contemporary equivalent of an idol is not a person or a thing but rather that our lack of trust and its constant friend, fear, constitute a form of idolatry. Fear of not achieving, of loss of status, of failure, makes us restless, dissatisfied, selfish, ungrateful, acquisitive and, inevitably, stressed. We are inexorably driven by a secular model of success, as is clear from the vast array of how-to-succeed manuals on the shelves of our bookshops. If only it were that easy.

'What are we here for?' Peter asks over lunch. It hasn't been bothering him unduly, he says but as the weeks go by and we don't appear to be making any useful contribution to the local community, apart from responding to Marguerite's now regular demands for company and support, it's tempting to wonder. Not serving any purpose is the Christian's daily dread. It would mean that what we have here might simply be a self-seeking venture and that would be very uncomfortable.

Is it possible that this very drive to be productive is actually counter-productive? Perhaps it's our definition of productivity that is at fault. Capitalism makes us see usefulness in terms of financial profit. That is a by-product of the materialistic age in which we live and places a heavy burden on its cultural subscribers. The ill, the destitute or even the retired, as we shall be soon enough, cannot then be deemed to be productive. Which is why, in the UK, following a lifetime of experience and even service, the elderly are often seen as a burden rather than a fount of wisdom, and became a target for abuse.

I remember visiting an elderly uncle of Peter's who had been a fine and much loved minister, responsible for positive changes in the lives of many. In his late eighties he felt regretful and useless.

'I can't cut any ice any more,' was how he put it. 'Though I do take every opportunity to serve God and my fellow geriatrics in the retirement home.'

As we sat, waiting for my train home, I grieved for this dear old man, desperately trying to find words of encouragement and comfort. Then I realised I had inadvertently dropped my ticket. There were hundreds of trodden tickets on the ground between the waiting room and the station entrance. Where would I begin to look?

'Oh God,' I heard Uncle Des say fervently, 'Help us find the ticket.'

'Don't worry, Uncle Des,' I said, reassuringly, 'I'll just have to buy another one.'

At which point, I stood up, set off for the ticket office then, on impulse, at the waiting room door, bent down and picked up a fairly pristine-looking ticket. It was mine.

Uncle Des gave a whoop of triumph.

'See,' I said, waving it at him, 'this is a little reminder from upstairs that you're not finished yet!'

Shortly before we left for France I walked to the park at the top of the town and became aware of the myriad tiny patches of garden fronting the endless rows of terraced housing as I passed them. Some were messy – a dump for unwanted furniture; some had been concreted over, some had been neglected and were full of weeds, some were over busy but others were thoughtfully cultivated and a pleasure to behold. An inner voice seemed to whisper, 'Your drivenness achieves nothing. All I ask is that you bring joy – both to me and to your world.' The problem is that some of these revelations are easier to file as pleasant ideals than to live out.

Saturday, 4th November

France is not conducive to a tranquil mind, not if you let its bureaucracy get to you. I remember sitting on a bus during my year in Paris, being told by an officious conductor that it was *interdit* to crochet. I was nineteen, bored by the capital's traffic jams and, unlike Florence

Nightingale, found this newly-acquired skill really compelling.

'Everything seems to be *"interdit"* in this stupid country,' I stormed back.

I am older and wiser. Good relationships are essential. Impatience achieves nothing. 'Chill,' I say to myself as we spend an entire morning sorting out our local taxes.

'You can pay for your water here,' an efficient clerk at the town hall tells us. 'And for your rubbish collection. But for highways and byways and the rest, you need to go to Saint Sulpice.'

'That's 25 kilometres away,' Peter says, which, judging by her weary expression, is not new information. She nods unsympathetically. There is no public transport system. What do the elderly do?

'And our television licence?' I ask.

'Saint Junien.'

'Forty kilometres away.'

The clerk gives me a withering look. She manifestly doesn't appreciate being faced with a walking Ordinance Survey map so early in the morning.

Somehow, within the continued exchange of pleasantries, it emerges that we intend to ask *Monsieur Le Maire* what one does about a coypu infestation.

'You'll need official permission to put out a cage,' says the clerk. 'And a licence.'

'So that's why the coypu won't go into our cage,' I whisper to Peter as she heads for the appropriate filing cabinet – with which the walls are lined. 'They know we're not legal!'

She hands us a form to fill in – then tells us she needs it in quadruplicate.

'Anything else?' She might just as well add 'while I'm so generously giving you my time.'

We think.

'Yes,' Peter says, 'I would like to dig a stream across one of my fields,' omitting to confess that he has already started the process.

Digging streams? Yes, that's definitely *réglementé*. 'You will have to speak to the Mayor himself.'

And if we build a swimming pool? 'Yes, that requires extra special permission, forms in twenty-uplicate and notices attached to your gatepost for several months.'

We make an appointment to see the Mayor and leave feeling slightly despondent. I am beginning to believe Lavale, that we are being watched by government satellites. No wonder he is paranoid.

'You've done it now, digging that stream,' I say to Peter, as we arrive back at home.

'I can always put the earth back,' he says sheepishly. 'Actually,' (and now he's becoming defensive) 'there already was a stream going through the field – in Napoleonic times. I saw the map. I'm only replacing it.'

Justifying breaking the rules, eh? We are becoming very French.

Sunday, 5th November

French cordiality is taken to great lengths. Everyone of every age shakes hands or kisses everyone else in any group they join – out in the square, in the doctor's waiting room, at work – and it can take forever, depending on how many people you have to kiss and how well you know them. For close acquaintances the process is repeated twice; for friends, three times; and for special friends, four times. The problem is deciding on the level of the relationship. Get it wrong and you can end up either kissing the air, or worse, nose to nose and mouth to mouth. I don't know whether anyone has done any public health research on French cross-infection rates.

There are so few evangelical Christians in France that a fellow *croyant* (believer) automatically reaches the 'special' level the moment they are introduced. The familiar *tu* form, not to mention copious kissing, is compulsory. Sevérine has three daughters, aged between eight and twelve. Despite the fact that they always arrive for church after the service has started, each child has to say a peremptory *bonjour* and kiss every member of congregation in turn. Manifestly, from the look of long-suffering endurance on their faces, they find it a pain. Their heads turn left, right, left, like puppets, their cheek barely grazing mine. It can't be pleasant with garlic-smelling, sweaty, stubbly old men – especially when they barely know them. And the germs we're all exchanging! On the other hand, it's impossible for people not to relate to one another when they're required to make intimate contact so quickly. And some of the English complain about giving each other the Peace.

There is a gypsy in church this Sunday and she maintains a distracting, high-pitched wail throughout. The congregation patiently puts up with her spiritual ecstasy. This is unusual for the French church, where divisions over different styles of worship are deeply entrenched. In France, disagreement is a national pastime. Small wonder that the struggling little French church, with no national organisation or structures and nothing to give any sense of unity, splinters continually. In fact, our church, with its eclectic mix of denominations and occasionally uneasy tolerance of views, is almost unique. But their forbearance hasn't stopped this particular lady telling her fellow travellers that it isn't up to much – flat as a pancake (because the people don't all wail and shout at once) and they haven't even got a pastor. Hopeless! Yet her very presence puts the church at risk. Any hint of untoward or 'sect-like' behaviour, reported to the authorities, could result in it being closed down.

Many gypsies in France have become Christians and, for the most part, have their own, noisy, very Pentecostal assemblies. But to help our little congregation out, they come to town every now and then to evangelise the locals – and only terrify them. Despite the transformed lives of the Pentecostal gypsies, French suspicion of traveller communities is as great as it is in the UK.

After the service, Patrick and Marinette invite us to a Chinese restaurant for lunch. When it comes to enterprise, the Chinese are the masters. There on the menu was frog legs chop suey. 'Delicious,' Patrick grins, weighing up my response out of the corner of his eye.

I opt for chicken (at least, I hope that's what it is).

Three of Patrick and Marinette's children come with us. The two eldest boys, in their late twenties, have bought their own farms next to their parents.' They explain that French young people don't go away to university. They live at home and travel to the nearest college.

'This is what helps maintain communities and the continuation of rural life in France,' Vincent, the eldest, explains.

'And that has great advantages for quality of life,' I reply. 'I miss my children terribly now they have left home.'

'Yes,' says Cedric, with a grin, 'but it's of little advantage when you're trying to find an eligible woman. My parents will be lucky to have grandchildren.'

'Who wants to marry a farmer these days?' Vincent asks.

I'm sure that's not true.

I ring my daughter, Abby, when I get home and tell her I have lined up a handsome Frenchman for her.

'What does he do?'

'A farmer.'

'Who would want to marry a farmer?'

Monday, 6th November

We have an appointment with the Mayor this morning – the most important person in the area. He is a tall, genial man, who greets us warmly in a cloud of *eau de* nicotine and points us, apologetically, to chairs in the busy secretariat. It's Monday morning and the room is a thoroughfare for people claiming back fees from Social Security for their doctors' appointments. They have appropriated his study.

Francois Mitterand smiles benignly down at us from a huge portrait on the wall. He has the rather smug expression on his face of a man who has achieved the position he believes he deserves. The Queen, I reflect, is far more pleasant to look at, motivated as she is by duty rather than ambition and far more durable. I'm glad English town halls don't have to resort to pictures of Tony Blair.

We have two main reasons for the visit. One is to seek permission to kill coypu. The other is to discuss the ongoing battle over our boundaries and to find out whether the re-digging of the stream that has taken up so much of Peter's time is allowed - officially.

'Of course you must cull the coypu,' says the Mayor. 'They were imported illegally by furriers around eighty years ago – but coypu fur proved useless, so they let them go and guess what? They bred. That will teach people not to obey the rules. Your neighbour, Patrice

Rougemont, is our local President of the Hunt: He has cages.'

'In East Anglia, where they were munching through the sides of the Norfolk Broads and causing huge damage, they've eradicated them completely,' we enthuse.

'*Hein*,' he says, unimpressed. He's never been to the Norfolk Broads. 'Leave me around forty or so. They saw off the muskrats. They too were imported for fur and a far greater pest. They built their little houses on top of every lake. They took over the area.'

We nod. How we're expected to save forty, given the coypus' breeding habits, is anyone's guess.

When we start on the matter of the boundaries *Monsieur le Maire* hits his forehead with his fist, then lays his head on the table.

We watch him in some consternation.

'Six years, six years!' he moans. 'Will this saga ever come to an end? But it's not your battle. You shouldn't have to pay a euro.'

'But our little lake,' Peter asks hesitantly, 'What if it's not on our land?'

'Oh, it's on your land all right,' the Mayor reassures us. 'Look.' He points us to a large, local map, spread out on a large table in the centre of the room. Manifestly much needed, it is left out as a permanent feature. We follow him to the table and he traces the boundaries of our property with his finger. To our immense relief, we see it includes all of the lake. 'Your predecessor – he's one apart. We call him *un caractère* – and that's on a good day. He never sought permission to make a lake and it would never have been granted but now that it's there, it stays. You are the lucky ones.'

'And I can reinstate the brook that feeds it?' Peter asks.

'*Bien sûr* – if it's on your land but I have a feeling it is on the far side of the public footpath and therefore the commune's responsibility. I'll see to it. I am in the process of clearing all the ancient walkways – especially the Black Prince's Way, which is right by your house.'

I must have looked blank.

'The Black Prince?' he says, trying to jog my schoolgirl history memory. 'The Hundred Years' War? With you English? The Battle of Poitiers in 1356? He laid siege to Limoges. Three thousand civilians were killed. Then he pillaged and plundered – and took all the land between the two towns.' So what's new?

'Like the current English invasion?' I suggest, with a smile. 'Only less sophisticated, of course.'

'Ha, very funny, Madame,' he concurs graciously. 'He was certainly very successful at undermining the stability of the French government.'

I can't imagine that was very difficult but decide on discretion this time.

'Your hamlet was his centre of command. He built a chapel only a few yards from your door. There were only a few stones left – it was my only historical monument – until about a year ago, then they got in the way of one of the local farmers and his bulldozer. My one monument! What can I do? No one obeys the rules.'

'I would like to create a sort of park area that the locals can enjoy,' Peter says.

'Very noble but don't be too altruistic. I haven't yet managed to persuade the locals to walk that way. Funny, your predecessor digs up the trees and you replant them.'

'We really would like to bring peace to the village,' Peter continues.

Am I being fanciful, or does a certain cynicism pass across his face? It certainly jolts his memory.

'You are a pastor?' he says. 'I heard that. There are two hundred English in my commune. Do you want to do services for them in our church? I am responsible for that too and it's yours if you want it.'

The Mayor is obviously surprised that Peter doesn't appear to jump at the chance.

'Too formal for you, perhaps?'

Peter explains that, being Anglican, we're used to both the Catholic and low church traditions.

'Always the middle path, *hein*?' he says, amused. 'How very English.'

He shows us to the door, shakes our hands firmly and invites us to drop in and see him whenever we feel like a chat, then adds, wagging his finger and smiling, 'Any trees you plant – not within three metres of communal land.'

'So we should have come to see the Mayor before we bought the house,' I say to Peter, as we leave. 'It's true. They do know everything.'

'Too late for "shoulds" now.'

I flash him one of those knowing wifely looks that is guaranteed to wind up any man, however longsuffering, that says, 'Told you so!' Then, of course, I spell it out. 'You heard what the Mayor said? Just what I have been saying. Leave the neighbours to sort out their differences at the Tribunal. He seems to think we shouldn't have to pay for any of it.'

Peter is not convinced.

Tuesday, 7th November

Another glorious day. I have never known a November like it – skies an iridescent blue, trees tipped with gold and scarlet, their long shadows stretching across the lake and fields. I'm almost tempted to long for rain, because until the skies turn leaden and the heavens open I'll never get Peter to stay in the house and crack on with the many bits of *bricolage* that so urgently need doing.

Watching him way in the distance on the other side of the property, striding along the lake in his shiny red helmet, with his red-handled saw in his hand, he looks like a Playmobil character. Round his feet the coypu are mockingly munching on grass, totally unconcerned by his presence, a mere two inches from our three cages. The carrots inside have turned green.

I cycle into the village just as the church clock bongs an ominous midday. The post mistress is not pleased to see me. A head pops out of an inner door at the sound of my entrance. Not so much as a *bonjour*. This bodes ill. She pops up at the counter a few minutes later and serves me grudgingly. This is a special favour. Her lunch awaits. 'Have you no change?' she asks, as I proffer a ten euro note for the one euro postage to England. 'It's midday. I've cashed up.'

My first real howler in French today – and I have to say in my own defence that it was more of a spoonerism than a language gaffe but that will teach me to share recipes. I was explaining to Marlène, who owns the Spar – she who makes strawberry crumble with chocolate drops on top – how I make a paté out of the smoked mackerel she sells me. I had seen the words *'pâte a tartiner'*, on many tubs of margarine and cream cheese and guessed it must mean spreadable. What I meant to say was, 'When you put smoked mackerel and cream cheese and lemon into your grinder, the result is a *pâte a tartiner*.' What I actually said was *'une tarte a patiner'* – a pie to skate on. I saw her struggle nobly to restrain the urge to laugh out loud, then she said impishly, 'I think you mean *tartiner*. *Patiner* – that means *glisser*.' That'll teach me to play the superchef.

Marlène was up on a ladder cleaning the top shelves when I arrived today. A big burly Scot came in and managed a very Scottish sounding 'Bonjour.'

'*Je suis plus grande que vous aujourd'hui*,' she says, look-ing down at him.

He looks up at her with a blank expression on his face and she repeats it. It's school French, a statutory GCSE phrase but maybe he slept through French lessons. He still doesn't get it.

'I am taller zan you today.'

'Oh, och aye,' he nods and stumbles on.

'I said it right?' she asks me.

'You said it right,' I assure her, 'but you shouldn't have needed to say it in English at all.'

'*Il fait beau*, huh?' she says.

The weather is amazing, I agree.

'It's always like that this time of year.'

I never know when she's teasing me.

'The summer of St Martin we call it. Only in this area. He's our patron saint and kind to us.'

'Fantastic weather for the time of year – very unus-ual,' says Monsieur Lavale, when he pops up like Mr Punch behind Peter, who is sawing hedges. He has obvi-ously decided at last that there is mileage in traditional French cordiality. 'I've just shot two of your coypu.'

I told Peter earlier I had heard shots but Peter said it was just the plumbing.

Last March, he tells Peter, our neighbour, Patrice Rougemont, President of the Hunt, held a regional coypu hunting day. Everyone in the area, men, women and children, spent the day grovelling through the undergrowth coypu-sighting and three hundred were done to death.

'Ah but the Mayor wants us to keep a few to keep the muskrats down.'

'Muskrats,' muses Lavale, 'I remember them from my childhood. They killed everything in their path – trees, shrubs, plants. They built their nests on all the lakes and sometimes they were almost two metres high, great towers of twigs and leaves and mud.'

This is only the beginning of his reminiscences of life as a boy. He tells Peter that water and electricity only came to the village thirty years ago. Just a short leap to broadband then, which has been promised for next year.

'My father,' says Lavale, 'was beside himself with joy. No more heaving buckets up from the well every day. He installed a lavatory, shower, bath and washing machine all in one go. All his Christmases came at once.'

Only he, Mme Delgras and another farmer called Nicolas Bellier, who lives in the big farm opposite, are village originals – here in the good old days. 'Henri hates me because I'm working in retirement,' he confides. 'He says I'm taking jobs away from the young and unemployed. But I never intended being a postman all my life. I always wanted to come home to my farm – when I could afford the financial risk.'

I suddenly realise how Henri must see himself: young, idealistic, socialist, anti-hunt, a crusader wanting to drive out the old and bring in the new. But manifestly no one else appreciates this.

We have a coypu in a cage again. I go with Peter to take a closer look. It's the size of a cat and quite cute, except for that rat-like tail.

'This one's docile,' Peter says, puzzled. It stays curled up in the corner.

'It's eaten two green carrots and a manky apple. It probably has tummy ache.'

Then it starts to snap and snarl, baring a pair of long orange fangs, throwing itself from one side of the cage to the other.

'I'd better put him out of his misery quickly. Leave me to it.'

There are some things a man has to do on his own.

I go to call on Marguerite instead. Today the doorbell plays *Au Clair de la Lune*. She's waiting for the doctor to call – again. The waterworks are still playing her up and she's going to tell him she doesn't want any more antibiotics. I tell her that I'm not sure he has any other cure for infections. But she only humphs and says he'll think of something. She already takes such a huge mixture of potions that she can't remember what to take when and relies on Bruno to put them out for her. Dangerous to give too much responsibility to him, I think to myself. All she has to do is wind him up once too often . . .

'What time does the doctor come?' I ask her. It's after six in the evening already. Most of the time it's after ten, she says. It's a bit of a nuisance getting out of bed to let him in.

We get onto her favourite topic – food. I have Patrick and Marinette coming for dinner soon. Do I want a brilliant fish dinner party recipe, she asks. Then try *lieu noir*. How can a fish be called 'black place'? She gives me detailed instructions for cooking it.

'Fish is expensive here,' I lament.

'Ah, there's a season for everything.'

I pause, wondering what this has to do with the price of fish.

'You know the Bible verse that says even the birds of the air are taken care of? Nature provides. I've eaten everything in my time. Fox tails, magpie but I didn't much like crow. Tastes of carrion.'

Then she tells me she actually made coypu *paté* and *rillettes* and stew and it's good. 'They only ever eat herbs. What's there not to be good?'

I remember I've seen chickens in the garden. 'Are those your chickens?' She nods. 'Food or friends?'

'Both. The little ones to cuddle. The big ones for Christmas. If I can catch them.'

Since I've never seen her do more than shuffle, I suspect they may be blessed with longevity.

'They know me,' she says. 'It's so funny, they all come to me but when I try to grab one to see if I can kill it, it seems to know that too and runs off.'

'And if you can't catch one?' I ask.

Then, she says, she'll be stuck with the wild boar Bruno has killed on the hunt. Roasted, not pickled in vinegar. 'And I don't like it roasted, bah. Give me pickled any time.'

I get home and look up *lieu noir* in a dictionary. It's only coley, thank heavens.

Abby, our daughter calls. I tell her about Marguerite's strange culinary tastes and that we have bagged another coypu at last. She makes the connection at once.

'I think you could go into coypu pâté production,' she says, 'if your chicken liver pâté is anything to go by. Or you could collect all the squashed salamanders off the road and make it with that instead. It would taste divine. Then there are the spin-offs. Coypu soup. Coypu stuffing. Traditional English Roast Coypu? Coypu flapjack.'

Now that's drawing a line.

Still no sign of our Atlas wardrobe. 'Ah yes, Madame, I recognise your voice. You have rung many times and we have promised it many times but it's still not here.'

'I've noticed. I don't suppose there's any chance you could find out where it is? This is now seven weeks. What's the manufacturer doing? Cutting down pine trees?'

'I'll call you back.'

She is true to her word. 'Next week for sure.'

'Which day?'
'That I can't say.'

Thursday, 9th November

Traditional English impatience – will I ever be free of it? Is that what I'm here for – a surgical impatience removal? A learning to live with more serenity? I have often reflected on the nature of 'life in all its fullness' – usually sitting in church on Sunday mornings. Is this it? Then why do so few of us appear to live it? I'm back there today with my reading in John's Gospel. What did Jesus mean by fullness of life? I found a Dietrich Bonhoeffer quote that I think may be at the root of it: 'Seek God, not happiness.' I have so often pursued happiness rather than God himself, expecting him to cough up and cater for my comforts. If I'm learning anything from the purchase of this property, lovely as it is, it's that the pursuit of materialistic goals doesn't necessarily add up to happiness or a stress-free life. Surely fullness of life must be about living more intensely in the moment, learning to hear, see and appreciate the multiplicity and variety of people God sends our way.

Peter went to the village for bread by car today, such was the inclemency of the weather, and was held up for a good ten minutes, as the Mayor and seven or eight other men were holding what looked like a serious committee meeting in the middle of the main thoroughfare. In fact, since everyone was far too courteous to beep *Monsieur Le Maire*, it took a fairly serious traffic build up of around six cars to alert them to the fact that their lengthy debate was causing a *bouchon*. Alerted by the unusual engine noise, they waved amicably at the waiting drivers and moved out of the way.

Then Peter noticed two police officers, an unusual sight in itself in our little village, pull over a decrepit-looking mode of transport that sounded like a bag of tin on wheels.

'Too right,' he said to himself, bristling with self-righteousness.'How that stays on the road, I'll never know.'

But manifestly they were far more interested in the elderly driver's papers than in his clapped out car that would never have passed an MOT *chez nous*. Not only that but at least four other policemen were all waiting for the pleasure of pulling the occasional driver over. It was a magnificent show of authority – in a village of around six hundred inhabitants that doesn't even have a police station.

'Ah, ha,' said Peter a few hours later, as we waited to be shown to a table in a Poitiers restaurant. At nine euros this restaurant's three course *menu de jour* of goat's cheese salad, gigot of lamb and *tarte tatin* was a very attractive option – and manifestly, not just to us. He had picked up a local paper to while away the twenty minutes or so we spent in the queue.

'A precious diamond worth over two million euros, stolen from a jewellers has been recovered from a village near us. It was France's biggest jewellery theft in years. The thief was a Belgian.'

'He was bound to be,' I responded, 'knowing how the French feel about those particular neighbours of theirs.'

'The Belgian police sent an Inspector to help.'

'His name wasn't Hercule Poirot?'

Peter ignored me and went on reading aloud, 'Their investigations led them only fifty metres from the Belgian's house, to a lump of concrete under a pylon. Under the concrete they found a small parcel wrapped in black sticky tape and string and when they opened it – "Bingo!"'

'Bingo? Does the paper actually say that?'

'It does.'

'What kind of journalism is that?'

'Bad journalism,' he sniffed.

'A local paper, obviously.'

'But maybe that's why our village was full of police this morning.'

'You obviously don't look like a diamond thief then, or a Belgian, since you weren't pulled over.'

We are shown to our table in an aura of English superiority, which is wiped off our faces when we hand the menus back to the waiter and ask for the menu du jour.

'Ah, it was very popular. You have to be early for that.'

'We were here early,' Peter said. 'We were stuck in the queue.'

'*Je suis desolé.*'

'I think we've been had,' I whisper to Peter as I look at the prices on the rest of the menu. But we haven't quite got the *chutzpah* to walk out and end up with burgers – at twice the price of the three courses we might have had. They stick in my throat.

The journey home is hazardous. A dense fog fills all the dips in the narrow country roads. Where the white lines disappear, it's almost impossible to see ahead. Bobbing in and out of invisibility, we finally find our home, its light only just penetrating a heavy gauze shroud. A ghostly owl hoots an eerie welcome. A toad is blinking hopefully at us on the front porch. It's a scene from a horror movie and we rush quickly indoors.

Sunday, 12th November

It is my birthday. I feel old, not grateful for the life I have. The latter is a discipline I am determined to cultivate, or I might end up like Marguerite.

We call to take her to church and wait ages for the door to open. She can't go today, she says. She's waiting for the nurse to take a blood sample.

'On Sunday? It's the only day you go out.'

She shrugs.

Since she started coming to church with us and meeting new people her emotional state has improved enormously. She is nothing like as depressed as she was when we first met her and this is medicine in its best sense. But a person's emotional well-being seems to count as much to the medical profession in France as it does in the NHS.

She seems slightly dazed. I follow her into the house. She makes a grab for the table and sinks into a chair. She can barely open her eyes.

'What are you taking?' I ask her.

'Hmmm?' she starts.

'You're still asleep. What drugs are they giving you?'

She waves a vague hand at the sheets of pills on her kitchen table. 'Painkillers and sleeping pills and antibiotics . . .'

'And anti-depressants?'

She nods.

'Marguerite, no one's system can tolerate a cocktail like that. No wonder you can't wake up. Tell the doctor he must cut the dose. He's drugging you. You don't want to feel like this, do you? You've got to tell him.'

She looks at me from a great distance through pale, blurred eyes, shakes her head, then rests it on her arms and begins to snore loudly.

Meanwhile, Peter goes to buy me a birthday cake at the *boulangerie* and is gone for ages. Apparently, he tells me as I leave the sleeping bundle and let myself out, the woman in front of him couldn't decide which *patisserie* to go for. 'That one' she said and as the shop assistant with tongs gingerly manoeuvred the work of art towards a box, demanded to know what it was called.

'*Mille feuilles.*'

'I don't want *mille feuilles*, I'll have that one instead.'

The new choice was almost in the box, when she asked, 'What's that called?'

'*Bavarois.*'

'I don't want *bavarois.*'

The shop assistant was apparently the model of patience. 'Is it the name or the taste that you're after, Madame?'

'Hmph,' came the reply, 'I'll have that one. What's it called?'

'That one doesn't have a name,' says the assistant wisely, slipping it quickly into the box and handing it over the counter, 'And you'll love it. One euro, fifty.'

Barry and Jean come home with us for lunch. They've been in France for six years and are about to move into a purpose-built bungalow nearer the church. This is a huge leap of faith, as they'll have to take out a bridging loan until they can sell their house. And with thousands on the market, how will theirs, lovingly restored though it is, stand a chance? Yet they feel they want to contribute to their church community more and, being in their seventies, over twenty miles away is around fifteen miles too far.

The contract had to be signed in around 130 places. And the detail demanded was beyond belief.

'Parents' names?' Barry asked the solicitor. 'We're retired. We've just had our golden wedding anniversary. What can you possibly want with our parents' names? They've been dead for years.' But don't try to challenge French bureaucracy, Barry warns us. It only slows an already painfully slow process.

At least they can reassure us that Monsieur Auneau's insurance policies are kosher. When lightning hit their dish last year, slicing its way through kitchen lights, the computer and the television, the bill was paid promptly. There is so little crime in France and so few claims that they are processed faster than *charcuterie* – the only thing that is in this country.

We tell them of our boundary problems and feel reassured when they say that our difficulties are minor compared to some. Apparently, a couple near them bought a house that came with a neighbour who walked in whenever she pleased and continued the practice with the new owners, despite many discouragements. When they then made friends with the occupants of a house several doors down, the neighbour was so incensed she wrote to the Mayor to complain they were planting trees within her statutory boundary. Fortunately the Mayor recognised the green-eyed monster and dismissed her claim. But not every mayor can be relied on to take sides with his English constituents.

I just wish we could work out whether Henri is the victim of local jealousies or whether he deserves their wrath. And if he is the victim rather than the perpetrator, what is there to prevent us finding ourselves being sued for all we have? 'Let your heart sink slowly and peacefully into your breast,' I remind myself. No point in worrying about what might never be. If you learn anything it must be that.

Monday, 13th November

It's my younger sister's birthday today. Even she is getting old. I can't seem to fight off the sense of despondency I feel at the passage of time. The weeks are rolling by at a frightening pace and I'm not ready to go back. So many issues I haven't yet resolved but they all seem to boil down to this – after fifty plus years, twenty-five of them alongside Peter in full-time church ministry, have I achieved so little with my life? The apparent end of my professional career, the reality of retirement, however soon or far away, force me to confront this fact. We are reaching the end of our ministry. Soon there will be nothing more to add. Is that it? Was it enough? How will we be remembered? What will we leave behind? Could I have done something different, something more?

What really shook me was a long chat on the phone last night with my beloved daughter and soul mate, who rang to wish her ma a happy birthday. As ever we got onto the subject of eligible men – or rather, the dire lack of them. I remind her again of the dishy curate I met before I came out. Jewish Mama that I am, I have been thinking of engineering a meeting.

'And is that what you want for me?' she asks tartly, 'a minister? After what you've been through? It's a bum job to wish on anyone else – especially someone you love.'

I am shocked – but Abby has never been other than frighteningly realistic. Have I ever had the courage to face what I really feel about this aspect of my life that rolls on so rapidly to its conclusion? Or have I simply subscribed to other people's presumptions about what the life is like? If I am honest, Abby is right. The life of a minister's wife is not what I would wish for her.

Peter was a schoolteacher when we met and married, yet there is a common assumption that simply by dint of marrying the man, the wife must share his sense of calling. I never did but felt that 'for better or worse' must constitute call enough. I was only vaguely aware then of the implications – the six-day working week, the marathon fourteen-hour Sundays from early communions to end of

youth group, the few free evenings, the end of any week-
ends away, the stipend (the Church of England hasn't the
nerve to call it a salary) that would barely cover the basic
cost of our heating, not having our own home (though we
could, temporarily at least, have a better one than we
might have expected at that time of our lives – even if it
wasn't exactly to our taste), the lack of privacy and the living up to everyone's expectations.

There was never, for my part, any sense of sharing in
the actual ministry. It was obvious by the time we left
theological college that increasing numbers of women
were becoming ministers in their own right and that in
all probability Peter would, at some point, have a female
curate. I was determined not to presume on any pastoral
rights or responsibilities, simply because I shared the
minister's bed. He was paid little enough as it was, without giving my services gratis. In the early years we
scrimped and scrounged to make ends meet, depended
on Family Income Support to heat the house and generous relatives to provide us with holidays.

As the children grew, so did my frustration – with the
lack of freedom and choices imposed by the relentless
hours and meagre pay. If I wanted a life at all it had to
be of my own making. So I invested in my own career
and, unlike my colleagues who went home for recreation, I went to a vicarage and Peter's work. Still it gave
me a sense of satisfaction and achievement, of being valued for who, not what I was. Now, when I think about
it, I have worked like a donkey, every hour God gave,
from morning to noon and noon to night and what do I
have to show for it? This house.

If I had my fifty years again, what would I do differently? Less career and more babies, possibly. I didn't
know how wonderful adult children could be.
Otherwise, not a lot. Whether in church or secular

employment, we have simply given what we had to give – and if that hasn't been enough for folk, I don't know what else is. But as I sit now, looking out over the growing shadows of the trees on our peaceful lake, feeding on the stillness and silence, I realise I'm not only not ready to go back. I positively fear it. It feels as if we have given our all and have very little more left to give.

Success, in church terms, is often measured in terms of bums on pews and a frenetic events diary and that is a heavy pressure to bear. Yet so much pastoral ministry is unseen and can feel like drips of water from a pipette into a vast ocean of human need. Gone are the days when the clergy had the luxury of time to visit the flock, dispensing benevolence and comfort. In a church of our size leadership skills can be more essential than tea and sympathy. And while leaders can be inspirational, few can be flavour of the month with all the people all of the time. It has hurt to watch Peter stand trial on so many occasions for doing what a leader must do – setting the course and direction of the ship, steering it confidently through dangerous storms, around jagged rocks and icebergs, bringing it safely through shark-infested waters – even if it sometimes means sailing so close to danger that it leaves bits of him wounded and bleeding. And he dare not defend his actions, for revealing what he knows can irreparably damage the reputation of another, putting them beyond repentance, forgiveness and reconciliation. He has to rely on a congregation's total trust but it isn't an easy gift to come by when all authority is subject to suspicion and hostility, fair game in a playground of equals.

Every manager has to manage, of course, often with few people party to the reasons for the difficult, unpopular or apparently high-handed decisions they make. The difference in the secular world is that the Chief

Executive goes home from work. They don't mix soc-
ially with colleagues. And they're not running an organisation of volunteers who vote with their feet.

There is a danger that the minister is reduced to being
a figurehead with no real feelings of their own. Few see
the agonising over major decisions, the hours of soul-
wrestling with God, the pain of confronting a friend, the
slow, patient untying of the knots that hold people bound,
the gut-wrenching sorrow of walking alongside a much-
too-young loved one on that final journey. Few take into
account the fact that we are not as young as we were
when we first went to Lancaster, but I know that what
Peter has lost in energy and drive he more than makes up
for in wisdom and experience. His gift of discernment is
more finely honed than ever. Sometimes I think the
Almighty has fitted him with a spiritual scanner. He sees
people inside out the moment he shakes their hand at the
door. He sees their heart, if they but knew it. Yet he has
learnt never to rely solely on his own assessment.

Last year his own heart held a protest. Sometimes that
involved a go-slow, at other times it went so fast it left him
breathlessly behind. The medical establishment took dras-
tic action and jump-started it – a procedure with a 45%
success rate. Fortunately, Peter was one of the minority.
Nonetheless, the hospital doctors were clear. This was a
warning. His ticker was not going to submit to such sustained punishment without kicking up a fuss. So what
changed? Not a lot, I reflect ruefully, as I look back over the
last months. What can change? The job, the expectations,
the stress? I might as well try and hold back Niagara.

We will of course go back and continue. For reasons I
can never fathom, we always do and that must be the
nature of calling – energising in utter exhaustion,
inescapable when uncomfortable, joyous even in pain,
all-consuming when we want to run a thousand miles

away. When else is it a privilege to drink such a poisoned chalice? And after all, the celebrity culture is erroneous. Popularity is no gauge of success. Leaders have to make some very unpalatable decisions that earn them few brownie points. I have been reminded of that by the prophet Jeremiah. Who, in their right mind, would have ever chosen his commission? 'I want to be a celebrity prophet, a glamorous leader, currying favour with the rich and famous.' What he got was imprisonment, flogging and being dumped at the bottom of a well. Dislike, aggravation and persecution seem to be the Hebrew Scriptures' imprimatur on calling and leadership.

We desperately need a new standard measure of success – dogged perseverance when under siege; faithful prayer on days and even weeks when God seems light years away; determined obedience when all the temptations are to do what we know we ought not to do; integrity and honesty; kindness and consideration; a commitment to justice and truth: in other words, living differently in a world that mocks our attempts at what is basic, let alone Christian behaviour. What used to be called fighting the good fight – winning a few battles on the way. Isn't it possible to do it – ideally, without ending up at the bottom of a well?

'Build houses and settle down; plant gardens and eat what they produce . . .' says Jeremiah. 'Seek the peace and prosperity of the city to which I have carried you into exile.' No heavy pressure there. A simple calling. If retirement is to be that kind of an exile, I welcome it.

Tuesday, 14th November

Lavale has warmed up, though now, when he appears, he struts around on our property like it's his. But then, he's convinced that it is! And what does a metre matter, after all?

He watches Peter digging his stream and is very free with his advice. 'Why don't you just ask Jean Luc from Bricofer to come and dig it out for you with his digger? At least he would make it straight.'

Peter represses a grin. 'Actually,' he says carefully, 'the idea is to make it look as natural as possible.'

'Ah,' says our neighbour, nodding, with a look of total incomprehension on his face.

The weather loves playing tricks on my husband. Having determinedly dug a one hundred yard trench across our field to drain it, the lack of rain means that the field is now bone dry anyway.

I cycle to the post office with an urgent bill that needs paying. My daughter's mountain bike is a boy's with a bar across it. My legs are so short that to get one of them over it, I have to lift it as high as a can-can dancer. I don't quite make it today and fall headlong into one of those lethal ditches at the side of country roads here. The French love a spectacle and car drivers slow down and crane their necks to stare. It takes me some time to recover my decorum and make it to the post office before the midday deadline. I arrive, just as the church bell chimes and find a tatty sign on the door, scribbled on an A4 piece of paper, '*Personnel en grève.*' No apology for the strike, no 'Sorry for any inconvenience caused to our customers' but then, no insincerity either.

I head for the *boulangerie* which also has a sign outside. Amélie has had her baby – a girl – and the bakery will be closed until further notice. That, at least, merits the 'aahhhh' factor.

I pop into the goat farm to find out what's happening. Patricia is rolling blocks of cheese in multi-coloured spices. She smells . . . goaty. I suppose Patrice doesn't notice. She says no one is sure why the postal workers are on strike or when it will come to an end but strikes are a way of life here and I'd better get used to them.

Amélie's baby is to be called Marina, a pretty name, except that since almost all French girls names have Marie in them somewhere, it seems to be pronounced Marie-nar, which doesn't sound quite so pleasant. Patricia is going to help out at the bakery for a few weeks, so that will be open in a few days.

'Tribunal on Thursday,' I tell her.

'Yes but you mustn't worry. Let your predecessor pay any costs. Do you know what he has done? He has only written to the Mayor to complain about my husband's hunting. My husband – the President of the Hunt.'

Her outrage dissolves into a wry smile and she adds, 'But since the Mayor is a distant cousin, he showed us the letter and we all had a laugh. All the same, the gall of the man. Let him pay your bills.'

'Hmmph,' I say, 'We'll see.'

Wednesday, 15th November

The post office is open today. But no, I can't have a new cheque book. I've too many cheques to use up and they won't give me a new one until they see the almost-to-last number come through. How do they know how many I plan to use and when, or whether I might not go on a shopping spree? Manifestly, the Post Office isn't the big spender's bank. It's very difficult to get hold of one's own money in this country.

I'm an avid reader of weather forecasts, though they're often inaccurate, probably because God knows it isn't good for me to see into the future. It only makes me

miserable. Still, I can't believe how way out French fore-
casting is. No one can really blame any Met Office for
getting the long range forecast wrong but tomorrow's or
even today's? Every morning, France *Météo's* forecast for
our area has invariably been 'heavy showers' for the
whole of the past two, glorious, sunny, rain-free weeks.
You can still read the forecast for a particular day up to
midnight of the day itself but by then they've always
changed it to match the facts. I have a feeling someone,
probably a cleaner or even the postman, arrives at the
Météo office and says 'Another glorious day' and a mete-
orologist looks out of the window and says, 'He's right.
Quick, change today's outlook.'

I also love the fact that the five day report may simply
have a question mark for day three or four, which is
basically, 'Haven't got a clue. Could be anything.' At
least that's honest.

Today the forecast simply said 'Disappointing.'
Anything less disappointing would be hard to imagine.
It is another caressingly warm, golden day – more like
an English late summer – and we set off on bicycles in
shorts and vest tops to explore more of the area. It's
good to feel the wind on one's skin in November and
even better, as we drive through the hamlet, to be able to
say hello to everyone we know. Henri's brother is
rebuilding the roof of a shed. His ingenious 'scaffolding'
consists of two tractors, each piled high with towers
made out of bales of straw and a plank resting across
them. Our neighbour in England paid three thousand
pounds for metal scaffolding for a one hundred pound
repair job on her roof. This is much cheaper, if a great
deal shakier. The French may lead on European health
and safety rules but no one would know it.

'You've got some work there.'

'Yes, must finish it before the rain comes.'

'*Bon courage.*'

'*Bonjour* Bruno.' He stops, pushes back his cap, scratches his head and grunts. 'Tell Marguerite I'll pop in later.'

And then it's *bonjour* from him and *bonjour* from me through every hamlet we pass. It's obvious who's English – and not just because of the cut of their shorts. They look like startled rabbits caught in the headlights when anyone says *bonjour* and are forced to mutter an uncomfortable *bonjour* back.

'That's an English house,' I say to Peter, pointing at a rather pretty white cottage opposite a large, goose-filled pond. 'Look at the name. The French never give their houses names and certainly not daft ones like "The House Near the Pond." I mean, you'd never have guessed, would you?'

'There's another give-away,' he said as we cycled on up the hill.

'What?'

'They hadn't bothered to get the French right. *La Maison Près L'Etang*? There was a *de* missing before *L'Étang.*'

'No there wasn't,' I said.

'Oh yes there was.'

And so I did that very daft thing all married couples do. I went back down the hill to prove him wrong. But he was right, blow it.

'Hmmmph,' I said as I puffed my way back up to him, 'I hope it gives the postman a laugh.'

Admittedly, some French is difficult. We pass through a hamlet called Haim. Now how is that pronounced? 'Ang' presumably, which isn't pretty, or 'Em'? I think 'haim', like the Scots pronunciation of 'home' would be a vast improvement. No wonder French is difficult for the English. It requires all sorts of oral and nasal contortions and guttural, gargling sounds that sound frankly rude. The English are just too sensitive and polite to speak French comfortably.

The fields are full of calves and lambs – an unusual sight for us at this time of the year. So are the bulls and rams that are left to mix freely with the cows and the sheep all year round and take great advantage of the fact. This is France, after all.

Thursday, 16th November

It is tribunal day at last. All night the wind raged, hurling itself in a thousand different directions, driving away the blessed interlude of high pressure that had bestowed on us the previous halcyon days. By morning the sky looked positively bruised and resentful. We set off after an early lunch so as not to be late and by the time we arrive in Bellac the heavens open. We sit in the car for thirty minutes, watching the pedestrians scurry for shelter through the rivulets of water on the windscreen, then make our own dash for the Tribunal.

It's an unwelcoming austere building. We climb the stone steps, worn by the years of tramping feet of thousands of little people anxiously making the petty claims that might make them just a bit richer, and tentatively push a rickety wooden door. We find ourselves in a dark hallway and wander down a dispiriting corridor to a courtroom at its furthest end. We hover. No one greets us, no one tells us what to do or where to wait. As 2pm draws near, officious legal boffins in black gowns and wigs, with dour expressions and important-looking files under their arms, scurry past us without so much as a glance. I accost one mid-way and ask for the toilet. He looks down his nose at me as if he has just noticed something unpleasant on the floor. 'There's not one here.'

But he's not prepared for a Englishwoman who has learnt not to be defeated by a post-childbearing bladder or the pomposity of little men.

'Where is there one then?'

He turns back, sighs and points out of the door. 'Down the side street.'

I realise he means the public conveniences. I have visited them before and remember a dismal, dirty little pedestal without a seat, only when I get there this time it hasn't a door either and is wide open to the elements and the general public. Things could be worse. It could have been a hole in the ground. So what the heck, none of the public is around and I'm desperate. I won't be the one uncovered with embarrassment if I am discovered. None of this business is of my making.

When I get back, the courtroom has filled with a motley of dishevelled, country-looking folk in dirty anoraks and brown trousers, nervously wringing their hands or chewing the ends of their thumbs. Can this large number of people all be pursuing legal retribution, or are they simply here for the sport? Peter paces the floor outside, his bright red anorak tucked underneath his arm. Just as well he isn't wearing it, I reflect, as I join him. It may not do to look like a robin amongst so many sparrows.

Silence falls as *Madame La Presidente* takes her place. There's a low hiss of uncomfortable muttering as everyone waits to hear whom the guillotine's next victim might be and then Peter's name is called out. At least, I think it is, though it's hard to tell in French pronunciation but the audience has turned round to look at us, so it seems a safe bet. I give him a shove and we walk hesitantly down the aisle together and come to a standstill in front of the bench.

'Ah, Monsieur Guinness?' she asks, turning the weight of her authority on him, ignoring me completely. I try to fade into one of the rows of pews, only the inhabitants are so intent on what will happen next that they don't shuffle up for me, nor in the next row, nor in the one behind it. I'm not prepared to reverse out of the court completely and force my way into the end of the back row. But the judge ignores the unseemly commotion and continues to concentrate on Peter.

He can't hear a word she's saying. She tuts and beckons.

'Approach Monsieur Guinness.'

He climbs the steps and, standing there before her, with every eye upon his back and every inch of his six foot three a public spectacle, he looks like a naughty schoolboy in front of the head teacher.

'Monsieur Guinness, we cannot proceed. The complainant's lawyer is on strike. Can you come back next month?'

'I'm afraid I can't.'

'January then?'

'No.'

'When then?'

'Not until June.'

An audible gasp echoes around the courtroom. This is beginning to remind me of something. I dredge my memory and there it is – a scene from BBC TV's adaptation of Dickens's Bleak House.

'But none of this is my problem,' I can just about hear Peter saying.

'Ah but it is,' says Madame the Judge with a slight edge to her voice. 'The law has commanded that your boundaries be established and French law is binding. Can you get a solicitor to act for you?'

'No,' insists Peter, as I internally cheer him on, 'we are not insured for that.'

'He could perhaps write a letter to the court with his instructions,' says a kindly solicitor at his side, who turns a benign smile upon him, which says, 'Another poor, innocent English lamb in a foreign field.'

'My neighbours and I have agreed to have them done *à l'aimable*,' Peter says.

A scribe takes down our address, holding up the court with her struggle with our English postcode.

'Very good,' continues the Judge, 'Then write to the court with your instructions. Au revoir, Monsieur.'

We are dismissed and walk out, no longer the centre of attention as everyone is waiting to find out whose case comes up next. The whole process has taken around two minutes.

'Patience,' I say soothingly to Peter, patting his knee, as we drive the 35 kilometres home. I know that black expression and heavy silence so well. 'This is France. This case could go on forever. Jarndyce versus Jarndyce, with the only winners the lawyers.'

'Not to warn us there was a strike and let us get all the way there,' Peter fumes. 'What do they take us for?'

'Tell me, even if we do have an agreement *à l'aimable*, why are we liable?'

'Let's just do it. We need to know once and for all where the boundaries lie. And Henri has tried to make it up to us in wood.'

'We're not here to use it,' I say cynically.

'It'll keep for eight years.'

'If we're still alive.'

Anger galvanises my usually gentle husband into action. The moment we reach home he heads out across the fields to find Lavale, who claims he had no idea his lawyer was on strike. Sensing Peter's mood, he agrees categorically to having the boundaries done *à l'aimable*, saving the cost of the expensive judicial alternative.

'Then get on the phone and instruct your solicitor,' Peter begs him.

'You ring him, tell him I said so,' says Lavale.

Peter does exactly that before Lavale has time to change his mind. The solicitor is desolate, he apologises, he almost grovels. The delay is not his fault. He is not on strike, the people who run his computer system, they are on strike and he couldn't print off any papers. He would be delighted if Peter would ring Monsieur Gehl and arrange for the boundaries to be done as quickly as possible. That way they can proceed to the real meat – Lavale versus Henri Bouvier, compensation for trees and bushes.

It is vital to get an agreement out of the Delgras too but when Peter calls Albert he discovers Jeanne is in hospital with bronchitis and a roaring temperature. Manifestly, Albert is not interested in his boundaries just at this moment – but do whatever you need to do, he tells Peter.

Monsieur Gehl isn't in. He never is. He's out measuring boundaries and he has a long backlog of court orders. So Peter leaves a message with his long-suffering wife and goes out to give Lavale an update on progress. He laughs when he comes back in.

'Want to hear the latest? Lavale says that Henri has already been ordered to pay the Delgras one thousand euros of compensation for knocking down a dry stone wall on the opposite side of the lake. I wondered where that pile of stones had come from. Not only that, he was also ordered to give Roland and Anne some land in compensation for destroying their hedges and fences. And, who do you think bulldozed the Mayor's ancient monument, the Black Prince's chapel? Yes, our illustrious predecessor.'

'Seems he is a real little monkey, after all.'

'Lavale says the locals are saying we should change the locks.'

'Henri, a hot head, that I can accept. But a burglar? I don't think so.'

'Ah,' says Marinette later at home group as I relay the supposed sins of Henri, while she makes the coffee and lays out her home-made walnut biscuits. 'But what have they done to provoke him? You don't know that yet. There are always two sides to every story.'

She is right, of course. Nothing is ever as straightforward as it seems. But at least, by the end of today, Peter's pastoral skills have convinced all concerned to agree to the vastly cheaper way of establishing our boundaries. And it could have all been done weeks ago.

Friday, 17th November

We rejoiced too soon. Monsieur Gehl calls and says he can't measure out the boundaries *à l'aimable* without specific written instructions from both solicitors. Peter tells him that Lavale's solicitor has already agreed. 'That would indeed be a miracle, Monsieur,' laughs the *géomètre*, 'a solicitor, accept a cut in his fee? Has anyone ever heard of such a thing? Since he takes a percentage of costs, that, in effect, is what you ask.'

'I didn't realise that,' Peter admits.

'Slowly, Monsieur, slowly. Be patient. This is France. It could take years.'

Peter admits defeat. There is indeed no reason to be in such a hurry.

We have to decide what to do with our fields once we go home – lend them to Patrice or Lavale to mow them for hay, or let them grow wild and see what trees might grow? We're not sure what responsible and neighbourly behaviour would be. There is no way we can let Henri look after them, as he has offered – not without antagonising all the neighbours. Peter goes to seek advice from Roland and bumps into Henri on the way.

'What happened at the Tribunal yesterday?' he asks.

Peter laughs, 'I was the only one there.'

He describes the fiasco in the courtroom.

Henri shakes his head. 'Don't tell me Lavale didn't know about the strike, that his solicitor didn't tell him. And he didn't tell you? Always so rude. If you knew what I have put up with all these years. The people in the hamlet, they hate me because they see me as a young upstart. You'll be alright. They won't be jealous of you – an incomer and an Englishman. But me, because I'm local, because I built a nice house, they can't tolerate it.'

He goes on to tell Peter that he offered to sell the disputed field to Lavale before he even built the house but Lavale didn't want it. And then he explains how he had to pay the Delgras compensation for a dry-stone wall he hadn't knocked over, after they refused his offers to rebuild it. 'I would never have knocked it down. It was so pretty with water cascading down it. But they wanted money.'

He offered to buy the tiny wood from them on the other side of the lake, as we wanted to do, but they demanded triple the amount it was worth. He offered to tidy up the dead trees, a danger to anyone passing by but they warned him not to go near.

'And on the day we first met him, I told Henri I thought this was a happy house,' I laugh, when Peter recounts Henri's outrage. 'How wrong can one be? But I can't believe the Delgras, that lovely old pair, could be at all malicious.'

Then I remember they told us that Nicholas Bellier blames Henri for his wife's death. Jeanne claims that

Henri harried her into an early grave – though she actually died of heart failure.

Caring as this may sound, there is an extremely pernicious side to any accusation that can neither be proven nor defended.

We have heard a similar story from Lavale. 'After his wife died they took Bellier's gun off him. The doctor insisted because he's prone to depression.'

'You think he would have killed himself?' Peter asked.

'*Non,*' says Lavale in the squeak he uses when he's excited, 'to stop him shooting Bouvier.'

'How does Henri explain Bellier's antagonism as well?' I ask Peter.

'Henri says Bellier had always been a tenant farmer, unchecked, doing as he pleased until Henri bought the land. Bellier bitterly resented any intervention from his young landlord. He can't even use the well in his own field, as Bellier would kick up a rumpus and there would be a public outcry in his support.'

I am reminded of Arthur Miller's play *The Crucible* with its frightening portrayal of how easily resentment and dislike can turn into a full blown witch hunt. Destroying the reputation of his young combatant is Lavale's only real weapon. He has admitted to Peter that Henri is right, he hides the fact that he is farming, so that the authorities won't dock his retirement pension.

Whispers, rumours, collusion, deception, jealousy and above all, the lure of money are a poisonous cocktail in a secluded hamlet like ours, where any moderniser would be resented. I feel the bile of injustice rising in my chest. Then something occurs to me.

'And our ancient monument, what has M Bouvier to say to that?'

'He says that all was left was a crumbly wall and it was very unsafe. It could have fallen on a child.'

'He could have asked for it to be made safe.'

'And it might have been done in another ten centuries.'

Our young predecessor may not have much sympathy with the Black Prince but there is no doubt he sees himself as a crusading knight taking on the forces of blinkered archaism.

Apparently French lawyers really are on strike. They held a huge demonstration in Limoges yesterday over the lowering of legal aid grants. English lawyers have apparently threatened to do the same – but feared it would spark off a day of national rejoicing.

Saturday, 18th November

Our gate has to come down. It's only three metres wide and if we are to have a swimming pool, builders' lorries cannot get through.

'No problem,' says Peter, as he strides out with his mallet. 'The posts are only a pile of eight lightweight blocks.'

What he didn't know was they were filled with concrete and metal bars. By the end of the day his hands are bloodied and bruised, his back is killing him and the offending post that has to be moved is only just beginning to cave in to his determination.

While he works, a procession of white vans passes him on the road above, tooting their horns and flashing their lights. It has the slow, dignified progress of a funeral cortège and manifestly expects the same quality of respect. This is the local hunt, a parade of serious-looking, heavy-jowled, elderly codgers in flat caps and green oilskins, with guns, dogs and a great deal of attitude. Within an hour the tranquillity of the countryside is drowned out by the sound of baying dogs, blaring horns and gunfire.

Given the jealousies in the hamlet we decide the new gate should be very low key. We don't want to look as if we think we are a cut above the rest. We only want to help local farmers keep their cows out of our garden. Peter goes to Jean Luc, our local builder's merchant, who says he'll be delighted to have a gate specially made and fitted in a week.

Régis and Claire, a kindly, rough-hewn Frenchman and his English wife, who are long-standing members of our church, make a pastoral visit to Marguerite, so that they can get to know her before we disappear. It's a very generous gesture to make the 38 mile round trip. She greets us in her dressing gown for the first time in weeks. She's not at all well, she says. She has to have an operation on her eyes. Not only that but she has a urinary infection again and since it won't respond to oral antibiotics, they have to be administered through a drip. The veins in her arms were too flat for a needle, so the district nurse inserted it into her thighs, which has left them bruised and swollen. She lifts her dressing gown and nightie, higher than might normally be considered appropriate in polite company, to show us. Inwardly I pray Régis is made of tough stuff. I don't fancy having to pick all six foot something of him off the floor.

Then she brings out the tea pot. She has never offered me tea before.

As we drink, we hear her major lament – the loss of her vital Social Security card. There's no claiming prescriptions charges or doctor's bills without it – and Marguerite has prescriptions. Régis tells her she can ring and ask for a new one.

'My fourth?' she asks in despair. 'The first two times they were nice to me. Last time they made me feel a criminal.'

Silenced by the reality of coming face to face with French Social Security administrators, whose reputation is legendary, we decide to turn over the room with her. I find spat-out date stones, dirty hankies and other unmentionables tucked into all kinds of corners but no card. We suggest she sleep on it but it doesn't allay her distress.

Régis opens the huge Bible he was carrying under his arm and invites her to read Psalm 31 with him. The psalmist knows exactly how she feels, he reminds her. He reads a few verses, then suggests she take over and read them aloud for herself. 'Be merciful to me, O Lord for I am in distress, my eyes grow weak with sorrow, my soul and my body with grief . . .' As soon as she starts reading she dissolves in floods of tears and can't go on. I wait for Régis to take over – but this enormous man is similarly afflicted. Claire and I catch each others' eyes and raise them heavenward. We resist helping them out. Both fumble for their handkerchiefs, then, with a mighty nose blow in stereo, finally make it to the end.

Marguerite is much more at peace as we take our leave, with copious kissing all round. The hunt cavalcade passes us on their way home looking grim, with no flashing or tooting and little evidence of any booty.

Sunday, 19th November

When the English lead services at our church, they try very hard to do it in French. A bit like learning to ride a bicycle, they set off well, then suddenly realise what they're doing, wobble, lose confidence and fall back into in English. Although there is always simultaneous translation of the sermon, either from French into English or the other way round (which is harder, since none of the French know English well enough), there is no arrangement to continue the process either before or after the preaching. So apart from the singing, the service can end up almost entirely in English. I suspect the French must feel left out. After all, it is their church and their country. But they are far too gracious to say so, or suggest a more all-encompassing translation. Besides, they love the support of English Christians.

'We would be so small without you English,' says 17-year old Emmeline. 'It feels better with more people.'

I gather that France Mission, which plants new churches across the country, while welcoming English members insists from the very beginning that no English is spoken. That may sound hard but unfortunately, as soon as the English are allowed to get away with not speaking French, they won't try. Before our marriage, we had friends with a strong sense of calling to France. He spoke almost no French at all and the learning process was agony. But from the moment he started to pastor a French church, he refused to speak English – not even with the English. I thought this was far too rigid but now I see the sense of it. If he resorted to speaking English, even with friends or visitors, it immediately excluded the French and undermined all he wanted to achieve.

The English do so enjoy being together – when they're abroad. Even if we can't be bothered with each other at home. People who would never normally rub shoulders in Portsmouth, kiss with a passion in Poitiers. We love to share the particular pains and joys of life in an alien culture. And English Christians do need fellowship, mutual support and community – especially in later years, when there is an increase of decrepitude, medical support and surgical intervention. But it cannot be at the cost of the French church.

It isn't enough for English Christians simply to think how nice it would be to retire to France. Joseph, Nehemiah, Jeremiah and Daniel were all strangers in a strange land – through no choice of their own – and gave their adopted people their absolute best. This determination to 'seek the peace and prosperity of their city of exile', has always been a grand Jewish tradition in the diaspora. That's why so many have been Nobel prize winners.

In fact, here in France, the English are becoming local councillors and even mayors. Kevin and Kathy from Essex, also members of the church, have started an aerobics class in the village next to ours, engendering many new relationships, not just between the French and the English but amongst French neighbours who have lived next to each other all their lives and still don't know each others' names. Sharing embarrassment and sweat has at least led to a progression from Monsieur and Madame to the use of surnames. And one or two are almost on first name terms.

'The French bring *gateaux* to share at the end of the class,' Kathy says, laughing: 'I don't think they've quite got the hang of the idea.'

Then there was a request for line dancing lessons.

'We've never line danced in our lives, but we said yes. We taught ourselves from the internet. And the team was the star turn at the village *fête* this year. Admittedly, the organisers were desperate.'

There is enormous opportunity to contribute to French society but it seems to require commitment, an inordinate amount of energy and ideally, at least a nodding acquaintance with the French language. Can we wait until retirement to come back permanently to take up such a challenge, before we're too clapped out to give our best?

Meanwhile, I'm not sure of the best way forward for this little church. It is so welcoming, who wouldn't want to belong to it? People care deeply for one another. Could there be two services back to back, one in English, one in French? They would never agree. It can't now simply be hacked in two, like the baby brought to Solomon. I now see why English chaplaincies abroad are so important. It leaves the indigenous church to the locals.

Meanwhile, the shop is currently still theirs to rent. Apparently, the owner regularly threatens to sell, then changes his mind, precluding any complacency. So the French members are working hard to engage with the local community and ward off any suspicion that being Protestant and small and meeting in a shop means they're not kosher. They are already planning the annual Christmas Carol Service, a virtually unknown phenomenon in the Catholic Church. They held their first several years ago in the Tourist office, a beautiful old building in the centre of the busy market place and each year, it has been packed. Vast quantities of free, home-baked, traditional Christmas food, French, English and German, went down so well that the Tourist office promotes it as a tourist attraction and now the church has to deliver, whether the woman-power is available to do it or not.

Monday, 20th November

Back to Limoges today – one last time, we hope – for the wardrobe. It is the inevitable flatpack and we won't need to borrow their van, if we drive with my holding the long planks of wood balanced between us, hanging out of the boot.

Wednesday, 22nd November

Thus far the wardrobe has taken Peter two whole days to assemble. He might as well have made it from scratch, in a manner of speaking. No two pieces, however small, have been joined and the instructions are in Danish and English. Handy for the French then. Looking at them, it seems the only option is to suspend Peter upside down from the bedroom ceiling.

At one point, as I'm painting the doors in the corridor, I hear a muffled cry, like a strangulated chicken, down my brush and find him lying on the bed with the wardrobe stretched full-length on top of him.

'Well, if you fancy that more than me, it's up to you,' I whisper suggestively, as I extricate him from underneath.

Finally, thanks to a mixture of extraordinary acrobatic dexterity and brute force on his part, we have a wardrobe.

Patrick and Marinette come for a meal, bearing macaroons, a speciality of Montmorillon. There is, apparently, an exclusive *chocolatier* in town, where you can watch the macaroons and chocolate truffles being made. How have I missed that?

They stay five hours – until midnight, despite good intentions to leave at a reasonable hour, since Patrick has to get up at what sounds like the middle of the night to me. They must have enjoyed themselves and I'm glad. They have so few chances of a night out. Marinette says it has been a rare opportunity to share some of the burdens of running a church with fellow pastors.

Patrick worked as an engineer for France Telecom (everyone seems to have worked for France Telecom or the Post Office at some point in their lives), before fulfilling his life's ambition to take on a derelict farm. According to French law, both buying agricultural land and becoming a tenant farmer require a qualification in agriculture. Patrick is the *propriétaire* of the land, the *agriculteur*, while Marinette is his tenant farmer. She was a secretary and took a European Union course in farming, designed to broaden job opportunities for women. Part of the farm is in her name, so technically she could be seen as the brain, while Patrick is the boss and the brawn. That was sixteen years ago and it has been gut hard work, not to mention a huge shock to their finances. France Telecom provided them with a reliable salary, realisable targets and an annual bonus for achievement. Now he is his own boss – and yet he isn't. He certainly can't rely on any salary. Success is dependent on factors outside human control. Taking on land that had known no care for many years was a tough proposition. It needed clearing, tilling and careful preparation on his part and the support of the elements on God's. Drought or flood, beetle or infection, could have destroyed months of hard work. For years he poured back his profits into the soil, to give it its best chance. He didn't dare go away for more than a day, never took a holiday unless it was a visit to his family in Alsace. Marinette has never been free to travel – not even to England, despite managing a very passable English with non-French-speaking church members who live in France.

And then the farmhouse was barely in a fit state to raise four children and needed total renovation. Yet, he says, it has been worth the hard work and toil, mixed with sweat, tears and prayer. Some of Patrick's neighbours have not been as conscientious at the slow, methodical, enrichment of the earth and the land has not yielded its rewards. They have less to show for their efforts, whilst his land has produced richer pickings than any in the area, even in lean times. And his two sons now have farms on either side of him.

Committed to such a labour of love, it's small wonder that for years Patrick and Marinette resisted the idea of setting up a church, losing the one day of rest and last vestige of peace they might have had. But as the land submitted to their care and the ancient timbered farmhouse with its oak beams became a warm and cosy home, they felt they had no choice but to recreate spiritually what they had already created physically. The cost has been immense. Over the years they have sustained a huge organisational burden, been responsible for worship, preaching, pastoring, council liaison and outreach events, often felt alone and abandoned, sometimes used and exploited by people who have arrived and enjoyed the benefits of a loving community, then left when any commitment was required of them.

'But such is the Christian life,' they admit ruefully, as we say our fond farewells. 'Caring for the land is an easy option by comparison. It's far more reliable than people.'

Thursday, 23rd November

Home group night and we are *chez* Hérique. It is a modern house opposite the huge HyperU supermarket, which must be very handy for him.

'I am from the Midi,' he tells me conspiratorially. 'We talk a lot, we are very emotional.' 'More talkative and emotional than the Jews?' I ask him. 'Well maybe not,' he agrees. 'Certainly not more than the Jews of Marseilles. They are so . . . in your face.'

'At last he admits it,' says Patrick, who being from Alsace Lorraine, which for centuries never knew whether it was French or German, is made of much more solid stuff.

'You and I, we have something else in common,' Hérique confesses. 'My family are staunch Catholics. They were heartbroken when I started working for the army and found real faith and decided to abandon my roots. My mother never spoke to me for years.'

'That sounds even harder than anything I've had to face,' I admit.

'It's still like that for many French people. Catholic loyalties run very deep. Doing what I have done can seem like a terrible betrayal. The priest may even visit a family where a child appears to have left the mother church and tell them that it's a disgrace to their family and community.'

But not in Montmorillon, I gather. At its very beginning, the church leaders had the courtesy to visit the local priest and explain their aims and now he is so determined to teach his flock the realities of faith that he has suggested joint Bible studies. That is a major breakthrough in community relations. The two church groups have been meeting together for some time and there seems to be a real sharing of hearts and minds.

On our drive home the Christmas lights are on for the first time, rows of them strung across the narrow main street – completely hiding the traffic lights. They are prettier than any I have ever seen in England, but you risk your life admiring them.

Friday, 24th November

It's Friday and the Spar is doing a great trade selling fresh fish from a barrow outside. There is no mass at the

church and not much evidence of faith in the village –
but eating fish is still a must.

I arrive home just as a builder's lorry drives through
the hole where our gate once was, with no effort at all.
There was no need to demolish the old one after all. And
there is no sign of a new one from Jean Luc.

I summon up enough courage to take some flapjacks
round to Patrice and Patricia's and ask if Peter could
have a word with Patrice about how to leave the property when we're away, so that the land doesn't become
completely unruly. They offer to pop round in the afternoon so that Patrice can advise Peter *in situ*.

They arrive at 2pm on the dot, very obviously angling
for a guided tour. I feel uncomfortable, given how basic
their old farmhouse is. They even have to walk outdoors
to another part of the house for a shower. But Patricia
ooohed and aaahed and despite it being beholden pri-
marily to France's equivalent of Screw Fix, declared it a
very miracle of modernity.

They then perch on the edge of our Ikea sofa, eating
my sticky date cookies. Patrice is the strong, silent type.
He says very little but since it was 4.30 pm when they
left, we couldn't have been too much of an endurance
test for them.

They talk at length about Henri, his complaints to the
Mayor about the barn they built and about the hunt, his
recklessness with other people's property, his reputation
for theft.

'We just don't know how to explain it – but people say
that young man has something wrong up here,' Patricia
says, knocking the side of her head. 'It runs in the family.'

They seem to be hinting that the locals think we must
have paid an absolute fortune for the house but they are
too polite to say so. They're not too polite to say that the
English, in general, are prepared to pay silly prices for

houses – or to suggest that we are putting property beyond the reach of the average French worker. Not only that but we come in our masses, do no work and claim Social Security.

This is difficult to refute. We know they are right – in a few cases.

'That's why we're getting this new law – no healthcare for the non-retired. They'll need insurance. It's only just.'

We had heard. It's a source of serious concern for some of the English who are trying to live out here. Shall I mention the French who receive free NHS care in England? Perhaps not. I don't know them well enough yet. I think to myself that this discomfort, being at the receiving end of racial criticism that is only just in a tiny part, is what it must feel like to be Polish in Morecambe.

Patrice promises to mow our fields for us. This isn't entirely altruistic. The hay will be useful for his goats.

After they are gone I notice two large patches of white fluff on our rug.

'What is that?'

'Patrice's socks,' says Peter.

I hadn't noticed that he'd taken off his boots when he came in.

'I think we made a bit of a mistake, sitting them on the settee.'

Peter agrees. 'They're manifestly more used to sitting around a table.'

In the evening we go to Ruth and Tony's for dinner. Ruth is working as a doctor at the university medical practice and what she says about the French health service leaves me hoping I shall never need to call on its care – though that, I know, is unrealistic. Generally speaking, standards are high and there is more financial investment per person than in the UK. But at the same time, there is no accountability required of nurses, no encouragement to improve their qualifications or stay up to date. Doctors are totally independent agents. Consultants can be as high-handed as they like. Ruth once accompanied Barry to the hospital to act as his interpreter. 'Interpreter?' demanded the consultant. 'Ah, *non*, I haven't got time for that,' and refused to treat him.

'He'd be struck off in England for less,' Ruth says. 'The receptionist was very apologetic and managed to get one of his colleagues to see Barry.'

Apparently many GPs run single-handed practices, with no supervision. A French Harold Shipman might go undetected for a great deal longer than he did in England. And they're a little over-generous with the medication. As a locum, Ruth once made a follow-up visit to a six-month old baby with a bad dose of flu who had been prescribed ten different drugs. 'I read up on the French health system before we came but nothing prepared me for the reality,' she explains. 'For example, a nine-year old prescribed statins for high cholesterol?' The elderly particularly are often given lethal cocktails of conflicting drugs. English doctors are not always as good as they should be at prescribing for their older patients – but at least they don't insist that medicines are administered through a variety of alternative orifices – by suppository or drip.

Ruth confirms what I suspect – that antibiotics are the general cure-all. There are now public health warnings on the TV educating the French in the dangers of taking them unnecessarily. 'Got a cold or the flu? Reach for Paracetemol. You don't need antibiotics.' Now I understand why Marguerite can't get rid of her urinary infection. When she needs antibiotics the most, they no longer work.

Tony has been trying to do some sheep farming – but last year, caring daily for his flock of sixty only earned him £800. Despite the high subsidies he can't compete with the New Zealanders who are selling their sheep to HyperU at five euros each. He managed to get fourteen euros a sheep, eight of which were government subsidy, and has now reduced his herd to twenty.

For a while he and Ruth let a *gîte* but there are now so many thousands of English *gîtes* that the business is in a state of collapse. And when they do let their small flat, it takes two of them around six hours to clean it afterwards. It isn't easy for the English to make a living in France.

A huge storm broke while we were there and we had a very hairy journey home, trying to avoid bits of tree strewn across the narrow country roads, not to mention two little Bambis playing happily in the road, blissfully unaware of the danger posed by a motor car.

Saturday, 25th November

Peter pays a neighbourly visit to Roland. Good relations are vital if he is to be the owner of the wood that all but touches the far side of our lake. He finds it almost impossible to follow what Roland is saying behind that enormous moustache of his. It is interesting how much we lip read without realising it.

Anne arrives with an armful of holly covered in red berries.

'*Joli, hein?*'

'Whose garden have you stolen them from?' Roland demands.

'I found them growing wild just down the lane.'

'No, you must have been on someone's land.'

'Roland, don't obsess about trespassing. I got them just down the lane.'

Roland sighs, then diverts his attention back to Peter. He's in the process of explaining the hunt. The leader sends each man to a different corner of the patch in an arc formation and there they wait while the dogs are let loose and flush out a deer, wild boar or a fox. At first sighting, a horn is sounded and everyone shoots straight ahead, not at each other. At least, that's the idea.

Apparently there is always one man at least who refuses to stay in his place, wanders off and fires indiscriminately. Bang, bang – and another tragic accident. 'If only we French were as well disciplined as our hunting dogs,' admits Roland, 'but we are an excitable race.'

When he hears that Peter used to be a mechanical engineer, Roland goes on to enthuse about his 'hobby' – restoring ancient tractors that he then sells on. It has taken us a while to realise that many French have 'hobbies.' Since the major French hobby is avoiding taxation, we're beginning to see how lucrative some of these hobbies can be. Lavale's keeping sheep in the field next to us is a 'hobby' with very nice subsidies, thank you. Hunting is a 'hobby' – but it just so happens that there's a huge black market in selling meat to the local cafés and restaurants. But then, as any Frenchman knows, it's almost impossible to set up a business of any kind as taxation and National Insurance are so high. If I lived in France, maybe writing could become a 'hobby.'

Sunday, 26th November

At 9.30 am the doorbell rings – unusual for any day but especially a Sunday. Little and Large are standing there, beaming beatifically.

'*Bonjour, nous sommes vos pompiers.*'

We can't think why the firemen are calling on a Sunday morning.

'We have brought you your new calendar for next year.'

It's a glossy, expensive-looking offering with a picture on the front of two robot-like creatures, their heads completely encased in shiny, black metal helmets, two deep, black holes for eyes staring straight at the camera, against a dramatic blazing background in ochre, gold and red. They are apparently *Les Sapeurs-Pompiers de L'Union Departementale de La Haute Vienne*. And I can only hope we don't have to use their full title in an emergency or the house would have burnt down before we managed to say it.

The two men nod meaningfully, smiling and shifting uncomfortably from foot to foot. From his long experience of dealing with gentlemen of the road, Peter recognises the body language at once. If there's one great conversational taboo in France it's certainly not sex, it's money.

'You English, you never mention your age,' Marinette once told me, 'with us, its money.'

Ouch, how many times has our true English embarrassment and understatement led us to apologise for what we have, explaining that we don't live in our own house in England, that this is our only home, courtesy of generous relations above and on earth. I thought their embarrassed smiles meant they didn't really believe us.

As we thumb through the calendar, the feet shuffling increases, until Peter finally puts them out of their misery with a ten euro note. We haven't a clue whether that's an acceptable amount but they seem relieved, back their way out of the front door, wishing us the very best of the season.

I'm tempted to say, 'and I hope we never have to see you again,' which is a joke they've probably heard many times before.

'Live the Daily Adventure' reads the caption underneath the calendar's team photograph. But Patricia told us later that one of the *pompiers* sadly hanged himself just a few weeks ago. This was very inconvenient as it was too late to withdraw the calendar and take a new photo. He was a farmer, Patricia explained: single, lonely and heading for middle age without being able to find a woman willing to lead a life of isolation, hard work and no holidays. Not to mention having to cook lunch every day for around a dozen farmhands, which Marinette tells us is what farmer's wives are still expected to do.

I wouldn't mind being one of her farmhands. It's shared lunch at church today – an opportunity for both the French and the English to bring out the best in their cuisine. Marinette has brought a big cook-pot filled with something that looks like cottage pie but its bottom layer – the meat – is much more dense and stringy. It tastes wonderful all the same. 'Ham?' I ask her.

She shakes her head.

'Beef?' She laughs uproariously.

Now I'm seriously worried.

'Coypu,' someone shouts in English.

She sees my face and laughs again, 'It's *confit de canard* – duck.'

Tinned, boned duck thighs, covered in puree of potatoes and a layer of cheese is apparently a local delicacy. Now that recipe is going home with me. It makes an English cottage pie pale by comparison.

Someone pours Régis a glass of purple liquid. He eyes it suspiciously. We English try to explain what cranberries are but no one can remember the French word for them. Once we tell him they come from the USA he decides to have orange juice instead. He also shakes his head vigorously at the pumpkin pie Susanna had made in honour of Thanksgiving.

My Banoffie Pie went down well. No one had tasted anything like it before – despite the fact that caramel has reached a zenith of popularity in France – in mousses, sauces, biscuits and even tea. 'It smells odd,' says Cedric, Marinette's son, 'I can't put my finger on it.' So he shovels it down his throat instead.

When we arrive home Peter is starving. 'How can you possibly be hungry after such a feast? Did you try the chicken lasagne? The duck pie? Kathy's wonderful chocolate pear crumble? The chocolate cake?'

He shakes his head repeatedly.

'What were you doing?'

'Being careful. I didn't like to take too much in case there wasn't enough to go round.'

'But this isn't England. There was heaps.'

I despair. I had repeatedly shouted to him down the trestle table in as ladylike a manner as I could possibly manage, to alert him to what was passing under his nose but as ever, he was so busy talking he didn't take a blind bit of notice anyway.

Apparently, Mike, a retired policeman, was regaling him with some horrifying tales of ex-colleagues who have bought property in France. Early retirement in France seems to be an occupational hazard for policemen, who then find themselves on the wrong side of French law. One couple became embroiled in a dispute with a farming neighbour over a tiny patch of their garden. Rather than face a legal battle they gave it to the neighbours, then found themselves being sued for the access to their property they had inadvertently given away. Defending their claim has already cost them over £80,000 and they're about to give up and go home. The neighbours, of course, pay not a penny. It's all covered by their insurance.

Another retired copper and his wife had neighbours renowned for a family quarrel over a barn. One afternoon they decided to burn their rubbish and lit a bonfire which they supervised with care. When they got up the following morning, their neighbour's barn had been reduced to a pile of ashes. A visit from the local police told them that they were the prime suspects in a case of arson by neglect. Despite the fact that the whole village was party to the ongoing family battle and that local people were in no doubt that their neighbour had burned it down himself so that he could claim the insurance, the English couple are now at the centre of a criminal case – with no insurance of their own. In a dispute, the foreigner is often at a disadvantage.

We have been let off lightly, it seems. 'Were we naive?' I ask Peter, as, later that afternoon, we set off on the Black Prince's cross country walk at the back of our house.

'Maybe we were a bit,' he admits.

'Yes but it's all very well for Patrice and Patricia to tell us that Henri had no business keeping us in the dark over the boundary disputes. On reflection, when the tribunal ordered the measuring of the boundaries, Henri had no means of knowing that it would take Monsieur Gehl over eighteen months to get round to doing it and that when he did, the house would no longer be his. In fact, had the purchase gone through just a few weeks later, when Monsieur Gehl finally came, the house would have belonged to Henri and he could have gone ahead.'

'Well,' admits Peter, with less certainty than I would have liked, 'when we have them measured in June, that should be the end of our problems. We haven't been accused of any criminal activity.'

We haven't, but the stories we've heard today don't fill me with any confidence.

Monday, 27th November

I love the way the French have managed to preserve the extended family. This Christmas, four and even five generations will share their meal together – and in relative harmony, because they are used to being together. They gather for a midday meal most Sundays and always on *fête* days. One of our neighbours, an insurance broker, even puts up a small marquee to accommodate his large family. No one sees family as an intrusion or a burden. In England, I fear we often do.

Land is important in France, because it is passed from generation to generation, giving a sense of continuity, even of immortality. These last weeks here, as I witness the strong family bonds, I have been thinking a great deal about the generation of my family and friends that have passed into eternity. I keep remembering the great aunts and uncles I vaguely knew as a child. I mourned their loss so little at the time. What impact did they have on me? Some noticed me, some didn't. I especially remember those that did. I liked being with them. They made me feel my thoughts and feelings mattered, even as a child. I wish they were still around to shield me from my own mortality, because, unbelievable as it is, I am now that older generation. Now it's my responsibility to become a doyenne that notices young people, that makes them feel loved and valued, that inspires them with a sense of self-worth, hope and courage for the future. I want this home to be a centre for family – in its widest sense, to make all who come, blood relatives or surrogate, feel better for having been. That will be my investment. How we are remembered after we are gone depends entirely on what we bequeath to the next generations.

This awareness of my own mortality has grown out of the oppressive thought that we may only have around twenty years in this house before we have to move somewhere with greater access to healthcare and the shops. That is not very long, especially if we only come out once or twice a year. Every visit will be a reminder that another six months, another year has gone. This home of ours is a giant egg timer. I'm so glad there's an even better home to come. Three score years and ten of life could never be enough.

Our pharmacy has a new poster in its window. 'Feeling ill today? Tomorrow could be too late.' And then – as an afterthought, 'Look after your health.' Is this a cheerful new government slogan?

Tuesday, 28th November

A flier arrived in the post. I knew it wasn't good news when I heard a long, strangled, 'Aaaarrggg!' from Peter, after his daily trek to our postbox which stands on our one remaining gate post. I go to investigate and he holds up the flier and reads, 'Public consultation on high speed train route from Poitiers to Limoges to debate the three options.'

One option, it seems, is virtually through the middle of our property.

'Why didn't our solicitor tell us this?' I ask him. 'She told us there were no plans to develop the area. Nothing to worry us at all. This, along with the little border dispute, seems to have escaped her attention. She hardly earned her hefty fees.'

Peter shakes his head ruefully. 'Actually, I did anticipate this possibility when I looked at where we were on the map. Fairly flat land close by, not too many houses – ideal for a high speed train – or a brand new motorway, or a wind farm. There are infinite ways to rob us of our peaceful paradise and the property of its value. Nothing at all we can do about it. Simply keep it on the open palm of our hands. We have always known it was on loan.'

I have been working on the flower bed next to the house, determined, before we go, to fill it with trailing plants. I fail to understand, when I have such a way with house-plants, why the outdoor variety gives me such grief. I suspect that gardening requires a brute force that all five foot of me doesn't possess. I can never dig deep enough to root out the weeds and I'm not patient enough with planting and pruning. This sounds vaguely familiar – parable of how not to nurture a church. I am just too small – or is that too feeble? – to be a minister.

It galls me that everything I plant disappears in days, and no sympathy from my mate. I will not allow my confidence to be eroded. I will grow for God. 'Give me today my daily Wisteria.'

Worn and weary, I deliver my tools back to their rightful place in the garage. He tuts as I crawl past. 'Look at the soil you've trodden in. I've just vac-ed the place.'

This from the man who wilfully trails mud across tiled floors, leaves mounds of French breadcrumbs under the table, spreads jam across counters, sprays the mirrors with toothpaste. That's men for you. No logic.

Wednesday, 29th November

We have so few spontaneous visitors back in Lancaster that we jump when the bell rings here. We are in the middle of preparing a late lunch – we eat much later than the French – at about 1.30 and when visitors do call, it's often while we're eating, so they watch us as if we were monkeys at the zoo. Fortunately, we are very late today and haven't started when we find the Delgras on our doorstep, leaning on their sticks. They have come to tell us they have spoken to their lawyer.

We kiss profusely, usher them in, ease them into chairs at our dining room table, wait for an end to the rasping breathing and hold our breath.

'Yes,' says Albert haltingly, still recovering from the exertion of getting out of the car, 'there shouldn't be a problem with a *bornage à l'aimable*, on condition that you pay half.'

'*Bien sûr,*' replies Peter waving his long arms in a gesture of largesse.

'We did this before with the rest of our property and it only cost 900 euros,' says Jeanne, slowly.

'Only 900 euros,' I repeat under my breath. A mere snip. And what's another bill amongst so many? Maybe I could use them to paper the walls.

She has brought some ancient papers with her which, she says, clearly show her ownership of the wood. She hands me a frayed, yellowing document, dating from 1881, the ink faded, the writing faint, and points to the relevant paragraph. From the little I can read, I can't quite see how it proves the entire wood is hers.

'Hmm,' I say, trying to muster some enthusiasm, 'what a lovely old document!'

Then she brings out an equally faded typewritten version her father gave her around fifty years ago. The wood, tiny as it is, must mean a lot to her. But at least, if it does, there will be no cutting it down – which is all we really want to ensure.

'When Roland inherits the wood will he *nettoye*?' I ask. 'Some of the trees are dying and look a bit dangerous.'

In fact, many are being smothered by ivy. The entire wood is overrun with bracken and brambles. For all their so-called love of it, no care has been shown it for many years. They can't see that from their house and they're not mobile enough to enjoy it. She sweeps away my concerns with a wave of the hand.

'The dead trees are yours,' she says. 'The live ones are ours.'

I have a vague memory of Henri warning us that was how it would be. But these two appear to be such sweeties.

Peter is describing the tribunal fiasco.

'I know,' says Jeanne. 'I've been to the tribunal twice and I couldn't hear anything. I went right up to the judge, to the top of the three steps, and stood there like a lemon. Can you imagine, a woman of over seventy having to do that because she's hard of hearing?'

'And don't you dare open your mouth unless the judge speaks to you and demands a response,' warns Albert, from hard experience. 'She'll have you ejected.'

As we chat a large black cloud of cranes flying in perfect formation overhead darkens the sky. The racket of their cawing drowns any conversation for several seconds.

'*Tiens*, they're late,' says Jeanne. 'They must be disturbed by the strange weather we've been having – still so warm. There's a saying around here that when we see them migrate, it's time to plant the crops.'

I don't know a great deal about farming but this much I do know – any farmer who waits to plant his crops till the end of November isn't intent on making a living, cranes or no cranes.

We remind them the boundaries won't be measured until June, when we return. 'Retire,' advises Albert, 'like I did. Everyone in France retires at 55. It helps unemployment.'

But not the economy, I ruminate. Especially when so many retired folk work tax-free on their 'hobbies.'

'There are no pensions for the under sixties in England,' Peter explains. The Church of England has run out of money and he won't receive a full pension until the age of 67.

'Impossible!' Albert warns, 'You'll be an old man like me. You'll have no time to live.'

He has touched a raw nerve. Everyone around us – many of them younger than us – seems to be retiring. It is becoming an ever more welcome option and that we can't really afford it is rather depressing. It seems unjust that a low paid job should inevitably mean a small pension – and that, like many pension schemes, the Church of England variety has had to be cut.

We must learn not to covet our neighbour's retirement. We made our choices nearly thirty years ago – but at that stage, of course, no one considers their pension, or the two years at theological college without any contributions at all. But then, we have so much to be grateful for – even if we will have to wait longer for it.

At least, Albert tells us as they hobble to the door, hanging on to each other for support, there's no need to worry about the high speed train coming through the hamlet.

'No?' Peter asks.

'Ah, there's such opposition, it will take years to build.'

'Why opposition?' Peter asks.

'Paris to Tours and Paris to Orleans and to Châteauroux is fine but why would anyone want or need to go to Limoges in a hurry? And why go via Poitiers?'

'But it will bring employment to the area.'

'They're all against it,' Raymond shrugs, 'because of the environment.'

On that strange logic we say our farewells until the summer. In the UK we need trains to conserve the environment. French townies manifestly have no idea that the environment they are fighting for has already been systematically destroyed by farmers in order to get higher subsidies for their fields.

'They're such a sweet old pair,' I whisper to Peter as we wave them off. 'How can they pursue Henri for compensation for a few bits of wood? What is this disease round here?'

It's Piccadilly Circus here today. As they leave another car arrives. We groan, as it's now 2.30 and our bellies are meeting our backbone, while Marguerite heaves herself out of the passenger seat of the car, crying. Bruno's eyes, as he gets out of the driving seat, don't meet ours.

'I thought you'd gone,' she wails, as she staggers towards me, 'and I couldn't find your telephone number to check. Why don't you come to see me any more?'

It has been four days. I explain that we have been busy, out, had visitors and that I did tell her that I wouldn't see her for a while.

'But I am so ill I haven't eaten for days.'

I notice her well-endowed frame doesn't appear any slimmer.

She begins to recount her gynaecological problems in detail, pointing at the relevant places and we bring both her and Bruno quickly into the house.

'Ah,' she says, looking around in wonder, '*Que c'est jol,*' but the distraction only lasts two minutes. She is sure she has cancer – in a very unfortunate place. I tell her I think it unlikely. The doctor, she says, pointing again with acrobatic dexterity, is giving her medicine that goes in here and here and here – which just about covers every orifice – and it isn't doing her any good. And now her family has decided not to come for

Christmas and Bruno, she whispers, making sure he is out of earshot, is a complete pain. Bruno, it seems, who is the only one of the pair who is civil and smiling, is having a good poke around the house. I am revising my opinion of him. He may well be a saint.

They refuse a drink to our immense relief and we finally usher them both to the door amidst promises to visit on Saturday to see if she is well enough to go to church. Meanwhile, she has found her Social Security card. Too late. Bruno had left it at the pharmacy. What she has to put up with, she mutters, making sure this time that he is in range. She has had to order another. And that will cost her a fortune.

Peter finally got round to writing his letter to the tribunal this afternoon, explaining to the President that we are not involved in any dispute and that we're willing to pay to have the boundaries done *à l'amiable*. If they don't accept that, then I'm sorry, French law is an ass and deserves to be broken.

Thursday, 30th November

Peter calls the Delgras lawyer – and we are back to where we were in October. We can't have the boundaries done *à l'amiable* as, tired of all the machinations by every party, the court has already stipulated they should be done the much more expensive judiciary way. But it's not all bad news. The cost is covered, apparently. It will come out of the pocket of the complainants, or the accused, if he is found guilty and be covered by their insurance.

Now this is beginning to sound like common sense at last. But if it is, why have we not been told before? This sounds just too straightforward for France.

Jon comes round to discuss what we should do with the land. He thinks we might be able to grow our own little wood on the west side of the house where the soil is rocky and poor. He suggests we just leave it unmowed this year and see what grows. We could find some oaks beginning to sprout alongside the road and plant them.

'The Mayor suggested plane trees because they grow so well,' Peter says.

'Do you like them?' Jon asks. 'That's the point.'

'Not particularly,' Peter says.

'Grow what you like then and don't listen to the Mayor.'

I go round to Patricia's to get the address of her electrician and tell her we have decided only to have one field mowed. She is not impressed. 'Hmm – a fire risk. Nothing will grow there anyway. It's all rock.'

I ask her if Patrice would mow the field on the other side of us. This means he gets all the free hay for his goats. She seems a little mollified.

Later that night, travelling to and from home group, we oooh and aaah like children at the Christmas decorations in all the little villages we pass through. Never is local pride and rivalry more apparent than in these impressive displays. Myriad lights are strung from lamp-posts and trees, around church doorways, over shops, along walls and streets and alleyways – in every colour and shape imaginable – bells and stars, holly and candles. Illuminated signs and tableaux that say, '*Joyeuse Fête*' and are accompanied by jolly Father Christmases, reindeer and sledge-fulls of presents are festooned across the roads above our heads.

The whole of Le Dorat lit up as we arrived.

'Clever,' said Peter, with awe, 'they must be on an automatic switch triggered by visitors passing through.' But since they switch themselves off before we leave town, we realise there is a fault in the circuit and they simply come on and off at random.

I have a strange dream that night. I dream that Peter and I go up to the top of the property where it meets Lavale's border, to the place where he has dammed the stream and diverted it into a pond at the side of the public footpath and as we study the huge coypu holes in its banks, a large snake with two small babies crawls out. It appals me that Peter has no gun and can't get rid of them. I wish I knew what it meant – if anything. Yet I feel it is significant.

December

I thought it was too good to be true. Peter manages to get through to Maître Poteau, Lavale's solicitor, who is as supercilious as a man of his reputation and standing in the profession could be, and reports what the Delgras' solicitor has said. Poteau doesn't know anything about the other suit and cares less but the Delgras solicitor is wrong. Civil Code 646 makes it clear that the owners of the property are liable for payment when a neighbour demands the boundaries be clarified – even if that demand preceded our arrival. What's more, Maître Poteau will demand the full judicial process. Of course he will. Lavale's insurance wouldn't cover anything else.

Poteau makes it clear he doesn't want to talk to Peter. Peter is not his client.

'So your client doesn't need to know when I'm here in the summer to have the boundaries done?' Peter asks, with annoyance. 'And he doesn't need to know that to have them done in June, Monsieur Gehl will have to be booked in April?'

The lawyer's silence suggests benign but bored indifference.

'No need. My assistant will be in court to make the arrangements later in the month.'

'Fine,' says Peter, omitting to tell him that we won't be there to facilitate the process.

It feels as if the time for cooperation is rapidly coming to an end. Lavale hasn't even had the courtesy to tell us that we're proceeding with the expensive, judiciary option. And I am blazing mad. We have gone out of our way to smooth the way to an amicable resolution. Since we are out of the country when the court sits, Lavale will find it difficult to progress his case. England tends not to extradite people over boundary disputes. Just as well. The English courts would be so full of poor, naive English folk who have fallen foul of their French neighbours that there would be little time left for much else.

We pop into our insurance company to see if boundaries really are excluded from our policy as we think they are. Madame Auneau, who is in no mood for 'Oh, no' jokes, is an efficient-looking, chic businesswoman, who purses her lips when she speaks and shrugs her shoulders a lot. She rings a local expert who confirms that there is no insurance for boundary disputes and suggests we get a solicitor at once. Our rights must be defended at the Tribunal, which is now set for December 14th.

'Welcome to France,' says the customer next to us who is taking out car insurance.

'Why should we be represented?' we ask. 'What rights have we to lose?'

She shrugs. 'Up to you. But I'm telling you what we French would do. These boundaries should be part of the *acte de vente* – the sale of the property – and we wouldn't have so many problems.'

Her assistant nods sympathetically and hands us a calendar as we leave.

What is there to defend, we ask ourselves in the car. The law says we have to do it. It's probably a good idea to do it. So we pay for it. A solicitor would simply raise our costs and then pursue Henri for damages. And we do not want more trouble. No, a simple letter will do. We are decided. Aren't we? We look at each other out of the corner of our eyes. What if there is some unforeseen disaster waiting in the wings?

'That dream you had,' Peter says, as he drives, 'snakes often signify evil intent. Is Lavale a snake in coypu clothing?'

The idea tickles me.

'Or he and Henri both, since there were two snakes? Or the innocent-looking Delgras? Will we ever get to the bottom of it, Watson?'

Saturday, 2nd December

The postman is a lovely, cheery man, who gets out of his van to shake our hands whenever he catches sight of us.

'You're not going?' he asks in some distress, when he sees Peter carrying a load of recyclables out to the car.

'Not yet – but soon,' Peter admits.

'I have to give you my calendar,' he says and rushes back to his van. 'It's thick, *hein*?' he says, handing it proudly to Peter. 'Quality. It cost me a lot of money.'

Peter decides we can afford to be generous since we're going and won't have to make a donation for the other 67 calendars that may end up coming our way. He only hopes we won't now have to kiss the postman every time he calls.

Christmas market day in our village. The Christmas lights are on in honour of the occasion. Stretched across the main street they simply say 2007. IIt's fine in one direction but looks like, 'ZOOS' from the other.

The market is a strange mixture of professional salespeople, selling imported chocolates, tins of goose paté and natural foot creams, and people with a craft or hobby they hope will make them a few euros. The latter are peddling anything from misshapen knitted jumpers with nobbly wool teddies on the front, or homemade beeswax candles, to oil and water-colour paintings that probably wouldn't get them a GCSE in England. I try some bland *pain d'épice* – spice cake that isn't a patch on Jean's gingerbread and some even blander biscuits at three euros a bag. The English are selling home-made cards – some a great deal better than others. It seems to have become something of a national pastime. What gives some of us the courage, or should that be *chutzpah*, to try and sell our amateur attempts at creativity at extortionist prices, while others of us would rather eat them and die of food poisoning than show them to anyone else?

The atmosphere becomes decidedly festive as one stallholder gives up trying to sell his rather insipid-looking *tartes aux pommes* and gets out his accordion instead. The smell of coffee is irresistible but I can't get near the makeshift bar. The French are there first. A lovely table lamp decorated with wrought iron flowers catches my eye instead. It's 65 euros – beyond my budget but its maker, a wiry toothless Frenchman with a gravelly voice, has seen my interest and wants to show me photographs of his other handiwork. 'I can see you're a lady who knows artistic excellence when she sees it,' he says, waving a pot of saffron under my nose. 'I grow it myself.'

The photos are impressive. He works in iron, bronze and copper and shows me pictures of a statue of an old soldier he has restored, fingers and all, in breathtakingly immaculate detail. Next, he shows me an ornate three-tier chandelier designed for friends who have a circular, three-storey staircase. And then his pride and joy – an elaborate nude in ironwork, whose curves and contours, mounds and bumps leave nothing to the imagination.

I am aware, from a sudden waft of wine and garlic, that the salesman at the next stall has been irresistibly drawn our way and is standing close behind us. 'Are you not going to give her a bathing costume at least?' he murmurs, over our shoulders.

'No, *la nature* is always best,' grins the little iron-worker, moving up closer to me, 'Don't you agree, Madame?'

My space is beginning to feel a little crowded. I'd forgotten that where sex is concerned Frenchmen aren't susceptible to ageism. Woman is still woman – however faded. In theory it's pleasant not to be dismissed as past it. In practice I decide it's time to make a quick exit.

On the way out I collect a small box of home-made truffles from the primary school children, who can't believe anyone actually wants to buy their wares and have to be nudged into making a sale by the all-watchful schoolmistress. The truffles look like plasticine balls. I try not to think how many times they have been rolled, or where the hands have been that rolled them. With a block of Patricia's legendary raspberry goat's cheese, I head for the car.

I should have stayed at the market. It's a long, hard slog of an afternoon, heaving branches of the dead oak tree several hundred yards across the field into our barn, so that they can eventually be turned into logs. Peter, meanwhile, is lifting boulders out of soil we have turned over and is taking them down to the lake to build a dam to prevent the water draining out in another flood. Or at least, that's what he says but I'm not sure why so many of his projects seem to involve digging streams or building dams. 'Oh, it's heavy work,' he huffs and puffs, lifting them into the wheelbarrow. I'm almost convinced.

It will be several years before the logs are ready to burn. I visualise us in our dotage – at least seven years hence – sitting in front of a blazing fire, appreciating the results of our efforts. Of an evening, there is nothing quite like sitting in front of a real wood fire on our verandah drinking Pineau, listening to the wind howling outside. The chance will come again soon enough. It's unhealthy and ungodly to wish away the years. Instead, as I have Lavale's field perpetually in my eye line, I try practising the old Celtic discipline of using the rhythm of my work to bless my neighbours and my enemies, especially when they are one and the same. I have just seen Henri moving bales of hay. 'Nice easy Saturday work,' he shouts across with a smile. How can such a nice man be pursued with such venom by apparently well-meaning people?

In time with my footfall, I repeat, 'Bless their comings and their goings, their homes and their hearths, their family and their friends, their crops and their animals, their work and their play. Remove all jealousy, deception, hatred and bitterness. And fill their hearts with joy.' Then, as an afterthought, 'Bless this land you have entrusted to us, bless its trees and its bushes, its shrubs and its flowers. Let the earth blossom and sprout as if an invisible hand were planting and sowing, tending and watering. And let many come and revel in its beauty and find peace within its boundaries.'

Peter takes me to show me his handiwork and, against my inclination, I am impressed. He has built a virtual dry-stone wall, strong enough to withstand a tempest.

'Don't stand there,' he shouts, pointing at my feet.

I'm standing about six inches away from him.

'Where?' I look down in a panic for spiders and snakes and take several steps back.

'There,' he says, 'where you are now. You're on Delgras property. That boundary was done a few months ago. And you are over the line.'

We both laugh but it dies quickly.

He tries the school-made truffles after dinner with coffee. 'They remind me of something,' he says, turning his nose up. 'What? Ah yes, plasticine.'

Sunday, 3rd December

We collect Marguerite for church, listening to the French National Anthem on her doorbell three times before she manages to gather her things, say goodbye to the budgie, call the cat, shoo in the dog and lock the door. She's always voluble and loquacious in the car – once we get her into it. It takes both of us around ten minutes of heavy exertion to hoist her in, along with stick, scarf, Bible, bag and umbrella. She sinks into the seat with exhaustion.

She married at eighteen, she tells us. He was an engineering student and she supported him by working at the Danone factory, filling little glass pots with yogurt – at a time, I chip in, when we English didn't know what yoghurt was. 'And we didn't know what contraception was,' Marguerite continues unabashed. She had three children and fourteen miscarriages in thirteen years. Even if they had had more information about contraception, it was too expensive in those days. The doctor told her that if she had another pregnancy, she'd end up in the cemetery. So her husband, well known in all the 19th area Paris bars, left her for an Algerian woman, then bled to death a short while later.

'At least my first husband was intelligent,' she mutters, 'unlike . . .'

'And the Algerian woman?' I butt in. 'What happened to her?'

'There was no will and the new wife inherited his entire estate, leaving the children and me with nothing. She was murdered three months later.'

Marguerite says it dispassionately, with the matter-of-factness of someone who believes divine justice follows her. It certainly seems to.

Bruno came along several months later. He was a farm labourer who worked for Henri's predecessor – a man wealthy enough to own his own aeroplane. At 36, Bruno had never married and yet he still took on three children between the ages of twelve and eighteen months. 'And they have always called him Daddy,' Marguerite says.

My admiration for Bruno increases even more.

'He speaks to Peter,' Marguerite says with wonder. 'I've never heard him have a conversation with anyone before. But he seems to like him.'

Church is full today. News has got around that the English pastor is preaching. He has decided to preach in French. I told him I would be his interpreter. I would be creative and that way the English would get an even better sermon. He was not amused. After the service, at that moment when the preacher needs a word of spiritual thanks and appreciation, all he gets comes from Vincent, who says, 'Your French was fine.'

We notice Marguerite is busy describing her gynaecological problems to Hérique in graphic detail. He's looking rather pale, so we take her for a coffee with Régis and Claire in what Régis calls affectionately the Paki bar. Most of the Muslims in France are from the Middle East, not Pakistan, so Pakistanis are something of a rarity and a wonder in a small town like Montmorillon. All the locals call the brasserie the Paki Bar and there is not an iota of derogatory intent in it. In fact, the two brothers who run it call it that themselves, and are integrated enough to be showing an overhead DVD of barely decent pole-dancing women.

Régis and Claire get up to kiss a very pretty young woman.

'Who is that?' I ask Claire.

'Her father started a Pentecostal church here,' Claire explains. 'But it attracted gypsies and a number of Africans. It got very noisy – a little bit wild, so the authorities closed it down. They used the excuse that the building wasn't safe. I expect there were complaints from the neighbours. That's how it goes here.'

'And the leaders haven't joined us?'

Claire shakes her head sadly. 'They don't go any-where now. That's France too. Very partisan. And we can't really afford to be divided.'

'It's getting a bit like that in England,' I tell her. 'Many people are dropping out of church altogether. They have their reasons but I'm not sure how they survive without a community, even if its worship isn't exactly to their taste.'

On the way back in the car, we end up discussing coypu, as we so often do. The holes hidden just under the ground are so dangerous, Peter says. He almost fell into one the other day. Unbeaten as ever, Marguerite tells us about the time she fell into a coypu hole, broke her foot in two places and spent two months in a wheel-chair. I love the French word for wheelchair – a rolling armchair.

'I'm going to have to get a gun if I want rid of the pests,' Peter says, 'but apparently, to get a licence, I need to take a course and pass a test. It's in April every year and I'm not here to do it.'

Marguerite snorts loudly. 'You don't need to pass any test to get a licence. I keep a .22 rifle under my bed. Call me and I'll come and shoot the coypu for you.'

The mind boggles. This little elderly lady, who can barely move or lift her arms and spends much of her life shuffling around in a dressing gown, firing a rifle.

'I'm an excellent shot,' she confides, reading my mind. 'Let anyone try to mess with me . . . and paff.'

I just hope I'm not around.

Monday, 4th December

Our last full week. I had a Great Aunt who regularly used to warn her family, 'Nothing lasts forever.' I have always found that hard to accept. I want to hold onto events, occasions, moments, people, but we must move on.

I draw the short straw – to ring France Telecom, erstwhile Orange, to terminate our dial-up. I wait around five to six minutes for an actual response and when I get it, discover it would have to be done in writing with a *'demande d'avis de reception'* whatever one of those is. I said, 'Can't I do it by phone?' Apparently not. 'And can't I do it by email?' That neither. France's foremost telecommunications system is still run on paper and snail mail. And we'll be lucky to get it stopped before we come back in the summer because there aren't enough staff to deal with the mounds of paperwork, especially as everyone retires at 55 and France Telecom hasn't enough money for both new staff and old staff pensions.

Peter meets Henri with a camera. He thinks Lavale has moved one of the boundary sticks Monsieur Gehl inserted when he was here. That is illegal. He is taking photographs as evidence. Next time, if I understand the local slang, he's not going to stand back. He's going to sue Lavale.

'This argument has legs,' I say to Peter. 'It's going to run long after we're dead and gone.'

Peter is now wondering whether, when Lavale told us Bellier's gun was taken from him in case he shot Henri, it was projected wishful thinking and he who would really like to shoot Henri.

'That's okay,' I tell Peter. 'We've seen Lavale's shooting. He'd miss.'

Tuesday, 5th December

We finally decide not to buy a television. Beating my old man regularly at Scrabble has been far more satisfying. Our guests will have to learn to make their own entertainment. The BBC website has kept me abreast of all I needed to know, which wasn't a lot, except for the appalling situation in Darfur, which no one seems to be able to do anything about.

A daily newspaper called *L'Echo* has been delivered to our door every day this week and that has given us a peek into French politics – at least it would do if we could decipher all the acronyms, dotted around every page. The French love them but we can't even work out whether L'UMP is right or left, or what FNACA, UFLAC, and AGEFIPH are. One of their columnists is the officer for the Departement de Consommation et Centre de Recherche pour L'Etude et L'Observation des Conditions de Vie. It must take him all day to answer the phone.

The approaching General Election means that political jousting is in season and the insults more barbed and frequent. Segolène Royal, the first female Socialist candidate, is the subject of much speculation – not all political.

At a meeting with the Lebanese authorities, she failed to walk out when a Hezbollah-elected member referred to the Israelis as Nazis. She claimed his comments were not translated, so she didn't understand them. But this is a major political gaffe. I have to say, as a Jew, that one of the things I appreciate most about the French is their whole-hearted and genuine enthusiasm for other cultures. It grows out of an absolute confidence and pride in their own. Insults of a racist nature are therefore totally incomprehensible, let alone unacceptable. Any others are par for the course. The worst Mme Royal's opponents can come up with is that she is a 'Blairiste.' 'Blairisme' is a form of Liberal Socialist mish-mash that veers to the right, then to left, in fact in any direction that might gain votes and popularity.

Wednesday, 6th December

Two smiling gentleman with beards, wearing smart suits and funny hats come to the door. I haven't seen such oily smiles in a while, think they must be Jehovah's Witnesses and steel myself for a 'Got what we were looking for already' conversation. But they're not Jehovah's witnesses – and they don't have calendars either. They're from my local friendly newspaper, *L'Echo*, which I have been receiving free every day, just in case I hadn't noticed, and now my time is up. They hope, after such generosity, that I would now like a subscription.

I can smarm with the best of them and tell them that I'm a journalist and I think their newspaper is . . . informative – which seems to make them grow at least two inches taller. I bite my lip in a bid to avoid any mention of acronyms. Then I explain, with great sorrow, that this is a second home and we won't be back until the following summer. They shrink back to their former size and tell me that I can take out a subscription for three months when I arrive.

'We talk about your Tony Blair,' they say enthusiastically, opening out a full spread with a large photo of our grinning Prime Minister. 'Look, here on page nine.'

'I had noticed,' I admit, 'and I appreciate the thought. But sadly, the sayings of Mr Blair are not going to tempt me to buy your newspaper.'

They laugh uproariously and with Christmas and New Year best wishes, leave me with their card.

The phone rings. Peter, waiting to hear from the electrician we have been chasing for a number of days, says in his best French, 'Allo, Gueeeeenesss,' and half terrifies Jean to death. That's the problem – you never know whether the caller will be English or French and whatever you say, in whichever language, you know you're likely to throw someone into confusion.

Within seconds the phone rings again.

'It's Marguerite,' Peter shouts. 'Bruno has killed her chickens and she's kept one for you. It's fresh and needs to be eaten, so can you collect it for tonight?'

He sees my stricken face.

'But she was out feeding them the day before yesterday. She loves them. She knows them all by name.'

'This is the countryside, my darling.'

I put on my anorak and amble round, filled with dread. I have a vivid picture in my mind of her feeding her chickens – in her dressing gown – passing from one to the other, speaking intently to each in turn. Which was mine? I have never eaten anything I saw so recently. What sort of state will it be in? Whole, with feathers, innards? I make up my mind that I may simply be bringing it back to give it a decent Christian burial.

I've never known Marguerite in such jovial mood. Killing chickens obviously suits her.

'We did eight yesterday, Bruno and I,' she says, handing me two bags, one with a scrawny looking, raw chicken in it and the other full of manky-looking sweetcorn.

'The chicken is for you, the contents of the other bag for Peter.'

She takes in my uncertainty. 'Not really,' she laughs. 'It's for him to give to the coypu. That'll attract them into the cages.'

'Did you kill all the chickens?' I ask in wonder, examining the contents of my bag carefully. It looks quite edible.

'No, of course not, not the babies. They're so sweet and silky, I couldn't do it to them. By the time I cleaned and plucked all eight I was exhausted.'

I'm glad, as I take my leave, that she doesn't call me her *poule* today, like she usually does. It wouldn't feel right somehow. Instead, she calls after me, 'It will be stringier than you're used to – no fat, fed only on corn. Cook it the French way, in a pan surrounded with potatoes and serve it with a nice salad, *hein*?'

While Peter 'winters' the garden machinery, which seems to involve moving lots of petrol from one tank to another, I set to with the bird.

'Good job the vicar's wife's Jewish,' I call to him, as I plunge a hand into its rear end. Chickens, I know. I had to clean and kosher them as a child.

The internal cavities are, in fact, amazingly clean. There is nothing left inside except the neck, which I remove with one almighty tug.

I decide that tonight should be our Christmas French House Project Staff Meal – our CFHPSM – for just the two of us, so made stuffing, leeks in cream and broccoli to accompany the bird. We usually celebrate the anniversary of our first date at around this time anyway. This is our thirty-second anniversary. There is no spare cash for a restaurant this year – just the house instead – a thirty-two year dream come true. As we sip the Beaujolais Nouveau we fought the waiting masses for in HyperU last week, we look around us and marvel. It still seems unreal.

'Just think,' Peter sighs happily, 'If we hadn't landed at La Rochelle Airport we would never have picked up the magazine with the ad for this house; if there had been no rocks in that field, the house would not be facing south; if Henri hadn't fallen out with his neighbours he would never have sold it to us. So many "ifs." It feels as if it really was designed for us.'

For pudding I had prepared two baked apples stuffed with honey and dates. Dried fruit is luscious in France – straight from Morocco, Tunisia and Algeria. We are in such a mellow mood however, that I forget all about the apples – until smoke belchs out from the kitchen. They are burnt to a cinder.

We finish the evening instead looking at Peter's photo diary of our sabbatical. There is the lake, his garden machinery, the little stream he has so lovingly dug, the lake, the stream again, the dam, the dam again and lots more machinery.

'Very nice, my love,' I say, stifling a yawn and head for bed.

Thursday, 7th December

So this is it – the truth at last about our boundary dispute and the bad blood in the neighbourhood. And I don't like it at all.

Jon brought a friend for coffee who has bought so many barns and farmhouses piecemeal that she owns most of a hamlet just south of the village. The problem is that Janice hasn't sufficient income to maintain them, let alone do them up. 'All those English watching TV programmes about the good life in France,' she says with feeling, 'but they never do any real research. Now they've swamped the market with their *gîtes*. And they've no idea what it's like.' One long lease tenant let her dachshunds pee on the futon. The last, only 42, had a massive stroke in the bathroom. She called an ambulance but the tenant died two days later. It has left her traumatised.

Janice left her PA job eight years ago because she couldn't stand the great British office for one more minute. She lives alone, does most of her own *bricolage*, keeps chickens and horses and firmly dismisses my wimpish admission that I'd be scared to drive alone in Paris in case I got so lost I was never seen again. She's tough, feisty and weather-beaten and I can't help but admire her independent spirit. Only one man has ever managed to intimidate her. And that man, she says, is Henri Bouvier.

A fair amount of her property once belonged to Henri's father. He was difficult at the time of the sale but she put it down to her poor French. On one occasion, his yelling turned him such a deep shade of crimson, she thought he was about to burst a blood vessel. But in time they established a pleasant enough relationship, despite the fact that she saw a number of her neighbours subjected to lengthy and loud haranguing by either Bouvier father or one of his two sons.

Next to her lived an elderly French pair, with little in the way of sanitation in their simple home. One day Henri, who had now taken over as master of his father's empire, phoned the old man and told him to come and fetch his cows off Bouvier land. The old neighbour came back very shaken and Janice claims that, when he removed his shirt, he was covered in welts and bruises.

'He beat you?' she asked.

'That's what this family does,' he confirmed.

Even so, she had no personal experience of any mal-treatment until the day she phoned the Bouviers to tell them their cows had escaped again. A truck arrived with Father, Mother, Henri and brother and one of the two daughters-in-law: which one, Janice couldn't say for certain. In what she claims was a jokey manner, she said, 'Don't let it happen again.' They didn't quite catch her, so she said more forcefully, 'Keep the gate shut. Don't let it happen again.'

She realised at once that she had overstepped the mark, saw the unmistakable flair of anger in all three of the men. Henri leapt out of the truck, pushed his face within centimetres of hers and began to hurl abuse and threats. The younger woman tried to drag him off.

Janice, trembling inside, stood her ground and told him to get out of her space, while the two women managed to drag him back into the car. Since that day, living alone has never felt as safe as it once did, not with the local Mafia breathing down her neck.

By the time she finishes her story, I feel slightly sick, the way I feel when a favourite piece of china is broken.

'This is the house that Bouvier built,' I say to her, looking round our sitting room, as if evidence of his misde-meanours might somehow make their presence felt in the atmosphere.

'His house?' she asks, shocked. 'I didn't realise it was his house. I think he has a screw loose. There's definitely something in the genes.'

'That's what they all say around here,' I confirm. 'But we have no evidence of it.'

'Seems pretty conclusive,' I say to Peter, sadly, after they are gone.

'Certainly leaves a bad taste,' Peter admits.

'Does it seem possible? How can we dispute first-hand experience?'

As I reflect on it, I think there have been moments when I have caught a whiff of latent aggression, a black shadow passing across Henri's face when he is riled. Or am I imagining it in the light of what I have heard?

'Remember when we first met him, how insistent he was that we didn't talk to the Delgras about the wood? We were duped. Perhaps it explains these petty litigations that on the face of it make no sense at all. Perhaps it's the only weapon at his victims' disposal. Like someone who sues the NHS for negligence because they can't get a satisfactory explanation or apology out of the system, local people turn to their lawyers and their insurance as their only recourse.'

Whether their attempt to humble the mighty Bouviers succeeds or falls very much depends on the outcome of our boundary dispute.

'Jean Lavale has said he only wants to walk the local lanes without fear,' Peter admits.

'My heart bleeds for him. In that case he had better start communicating with us, not hand us over to his vulture of a lawyer.'

Peter nods. 'If the bushes Henri destroyed do turn out to be on Lavale's land, we can't trust him either not to sue us for reparation.'

Nonetheless, I fear I may have wronged Patricia and the rest of our neighbours for not understanding their fear. 'Perhaps that's why we are here, to try and bring some resolution, some peace – if that isn't too presumptuous.'

Peter smiles.'At least we haven't a neighbour, who, if they're not exactly glad to see the English, doesn't think we're a great improvement on what was before us.'

Saturday, 9th December

I feel I ought to know what everyone in England is wearing this winter, so that I don't look a dowdy vicar's wife when I get home. I take a look at Per Una and Monsoon's websites but can't get excited about what they have to offer. Maybe I'm cured – delivered from my shopping addiction. I haven't bought clothes for three months and have no desire to do so. Slobbing around in the same two pairs of cargo pants for all these weeks has saved me. We might even be able to pay the mortgage at this rate.

Patricia is going to send on our post. As I address and stamp envelopes for her, I am struck by the amount of work involved in having a property abroad. It is taking days to pack away machinery and do all the paperwork – precious days that will come out of our holidays in future. And the expense seems unending. The more possessions we have, the more complex our lives, the less time we have for the things that matter.

Packing is an endurance test when you have a man like mine. He writes long lists of things to do that never come to an end. It has bewildered me for years, until I finally work it out. Each time an item is crossed off, he adds two more – usually something to do with machines or making dams. And then, just when I have swept and washed the floors, he swats a huge fly that leaves a trail of gooey mush and I have to start all over again. Marriage should make saints out of us.

Jean Luc arrives with our gate – only three weeks late, which is a record for a Frenchman. Peter reminded him three days ago that our departure is imminent and the shock of it seems to have galvanised him into action.

He brings a double, not the single gate we ordered. 'Ah, Monsieur Guinness,' he says apologetically, 'I couldn't make you a farm gate. It wouldn't be right. A property like this, it needs a double gate. So I made you something much nicer – much more fitting.'

We pay up without complaining. You can't argue with a Frenchman's good taste. He has his pride after all.

Sunday, 10th December

It's a grey, foggy day, the mist that drapes the hills and trees hanging over our spirits.

It is our last visit to the church in Montmorillon. I translate for Patrick, which is an interesting experience as I don't quite agree with what he said about humans being mind, body and spirit. That's a very Greek idea and not in Hebraic thinking, where human beings are a unified whole. It reinforces the erroneous notion that the spiritual is more important than the physical and implies that they are not as interconnected as they actually are. I am tempted to preach my own sermon, then note the warning look from Peter as he sits in the congregation and decide to stay true to the preacher. It isn't easy to catch the nuances of the sermon, rather than simply be accurate to the words.

Everyone kisses us goodbye at length and tells us that meeting us has truly been *'un grand plaisir'* and how they wish we could stay forever.

'Remember, we are sheep without a shepherd,' Barry says to Peter with meaning as we leave. We know it and it tugs at our hearts. We finally stumble out of the door inundated with cards and yet another calendar – full of photos of the young people. That calendar I will keep. It will go on my toilet wall, along with the photographs of everyone I love and pray for. I have to go in there several times a day. It might as well be a useful spiritual experience. That is where body and spirit meet.

I'm really not looking forward to going home – battling my way through heavy traffic and our heaving, one-way system, to packed supermarkets with no parking spaces, to canned Christmas music and English bad temper. I can't muster up any enthusiasm for any of it.

And have we really learnt to fight the battle of busyness, or will we simply jump back on the treadmill, as if these months had never happened? The church is like the rest of society – ruled by financial constraints. Dioceses are cutting costs by cutting clergy. Yet expectations are as high as ever – that the minister or pastor will visit all, preach well, be constructive, visionary, creative and high-tech.

We have not yet discovered any real solutions to the problem. Jesus was often so busy he didn't have time to eat. He escaped from time to time to refuel, to have more to offer the people who needed him. We have certainly decided to be more disciplined in creating times of 'escape.' We have experienced the reality of the man who stopped to sharpen his axe and cut far more logs than the man who went at it from morning till night without a break.

Perhaps even more radical action is required. Should we switch off the big wheel, stop all our busy church programmes, drop out of the mainstream and develop cell or home church? We certainly need to discover a new way of *being*, not *doing* church. The NHS subscribes to the principle of evidence-based medicine and treatment, whether it actually adheres to it or not. Clinicians should be able to produce the research that proves their methods are effective. But the church does little research and appears to have little evidence to justify anything it does. Perhaps people have to contend with so much change in the workplace that the church inadvertently becomes their rock of unchangeability.

We set off to the goat farm to give Patrice and Patricia a door key and key to our postbox but they arrive just as we're leaving. I'm glad they weren't put off by their last visit which was so stiff and formal. In fact they're much more relaxed this time and have Mark, their son and would-be master pâtissier with them. I'm even brave enough to serve some home-made tray bakes.

In fact, they're so relaxed they stay two hours – just as we were covering everything in dust sheets. Arrrgh, so much for an early night. However, they do tell us a very interesting tale about our neighbour Lavale, or Jeannot as they call him. Peter thought they called him Jeannot because they were close. I think it's more likely to be derogatory – the equivalent of calling Charles a proper Charlie.

When they bought the farm they decided to enlarge the drive for their lorries, so Patrice checked the boundaries he had been given and marked them with posts, ensuring that the tractor would stay well clear of Lavale's property. One day, as Patricia was looking out of her kitchen window, she saw Jeannot creep up, look all around him like a squirrel, then furtively remove the post from the ground and move it several feet further in. Suddenly he jumped, ran down the road as fast as his little legs would carry him and disappeared from sight, just as Patrice's blue van pulled into the drive. Patricia said it was one of the funniest things she had seen.

Patrice went to find him and said, 'Jean, if you have a problem with my understanding of our boundary, call the *géomètre* and we'll sort it out.' He who calls the *géomètre* pays the bill, so Jeannot never quite got round to it and the drive was extended as Patrice intended.

'Leave your neighbours to it,' Patricia advised. 'They've been fighting over the boundaries for six years already and they'll go on fighting for another six at least. That's what they're like. Put together an obsessional like Jeannot and a young hothead like Bouvier and it's inevitable.'

Monday, 11th December

Peter goes to collect the bread from the *boulangerie* one last time and comes back with chocolates from Patricia and from Marlène at the Spar and a home-made brioche from Amélie, the baker's wife, who is now back at work with a baby on her back.

'Be sure to tell Michele that Mark says the million-aire's shortbread she gave us is very good,' Patricia tells Peter. Praise from her master-pastry chef son is praise indeed.

As I look at these small tokens of love and affection, I reflect that during our three months, though we have become rich in material gifts, we are even richer in new friendships and that they are of far more worth than a house. I never settle anywhere without a struggle. I thought I would never be able to cope with living abroad permanently. Now I think I can.

As I make one last call on Marguerite, the doorbell plays a surprise, '*Happy Birthday to You.*' She is fully dressed, not in a dressing gown. She's even wearing a little make-up. And she is smiling. She holds out a bunch of holly she has picked specially for us and we both go, 'oooh, ouch' as she hands it to me and the spines find their way into our skin. I tell her Jon has agreed to take her to church next week but he wants to stay on for the Christmas meal.

'For once, why don't you stay too?' I suggest.

'I can't, I can't,' she says in near panic, 'I'm not well, I have to have an eye operation, I can't stand for long . . . and there is Bruno.'

I suspected she was quite obsessive about giving Bruno his lunch every day.

'Ah, that's what this is about – Bruno! Would he give up lunch out for you? You know he wouldn't. Did he take you with him last week when he went to the communal pensioners' Christmas lunch? No, he didn't. Some festive goodwill and cheer. You need to live, to manage without him.'

Something in her eyes suddenly clears. The panic recedes like the tide. She smiles.

'You may be right. I'll think about it.'

She kisses me profusely, then calls after me, 'You won't forget me? You will write?'

I promise I will.

'I feel so much better since you and Peter arrived here. What will life be without you?'

There's no answer to that, so I rush away before the hanky reaches her eyes.

Tuesday, 12th December

Our sabbatical is at an end. In the car, on the way to Calais, like the well-trained professionals we're supposed to be, we review our goals to see whether they have been achieved: to rest, study, make contact with the

French Church, prepare for retirement and see whether we could live here permanently as useful citizens. Hurrah, we can tick all the boxes.

There's just one problem. That seems to have generated a new set of issues. We did finally rest – once the stress of setting up home was overcome. We studied, a routine was established and, with British forbearance, we finally adapted to life without marmalade and ginger nuts and to the oft-incomprehensible ways of our neighbours over the Channel. In fact, we have integrated so well that leaving tears us in two and now, it seems, we shall be forever plagued by the emotional tug-of-war of people who yo-yo between two communities, part of themselves always somewhere else.

Unearthing the French Church has been a huge challenge. The total self-giving of around four or five key couples is truly astonishing. None pretended that planting the first Protestant church was going to be easy but nor did they anticipate the full cost of the past five years – chasing half way across France to intercede with the local authorities on behalf of illegal immigrants who, with a new name, then vanished into the ether; financing out of their own pockets the African relatives of church members who come for medical treatment and can neither afford it nor the fare home; organising wedding parties for impecunious couples who disappear within weeks with different partners; painfully nurturing faith in local people frightened of bringing down the wrath of their priest; interpreting for a motley band of non-French speaking Baptist, Methodist, Pentecostal and Anglican English, who then decide it's not their thing; putting up with the disruption of worship by noisy gypsies who then complain their services are far too dull to be endured; and constantly running the risk of a visit from the police if they are reported as a sect.

Will they even have a building when we come back in the summer? In other words, they have twice the frustration, aggravation and sacrifice of ministry, without a stipend and on top of a demanding secular job.

We can't pretend the worship is aesthetically pleasing. Instrumental accompaniment may be reduced to a single recorder or saxophone, depending on who does or doesn't turn up, and it's often staccato, as players scramble for sheets of music or retune their instruments. But we realise we could have plenty of beautifully crafted worship in the UK, without the heart. They are begging us to stay and of course there's a pull when the need is so great. But leaving Lancaster, which has been our life for the past fifteen years, would be an even greater wrench just at this moment.

The *Daily Telegraph* reports that emigration from Britain has never been so high. Australia is the preferred destination, followed by France. At least sixty thousand people a year are investing in the French rather than the British economy. They lament an erosion of the 'old' values – honesty, simplicity, family and community. They resent overcrowding. They blame successive governments for failing to address these key issues. Yet many, though they find the new life they think they want, still feel that something is missing and are looking for whatever it is.

I have reached the book of Revelation and, reading some background to this complex book, discover that the Christian church then was either persecuted and martyred or subsumed in the prevailing culture of success. The writer, John speaks of eternal rewards for the former. But the latter will not escape the financial disasters that threaten every culture based on wealth. Our economy has never been so volatile. Stock markets are fragile, often dependent on the whims or greed of one or two individuals. The housing market is wobbly. We must hold all we have, even our new home, on an open hand and invest in people instead.

We popped in on the Mayor to say goodbye just before we left, to check he will be as good as his word when it comes to digging out the proper source for the stream at the top of our field.

'Of course,' he says, waving away the billowing waft of cigarette smoke he has just exhaled. 'You can count on me.'

We're not so sure we can count on any job being done before the second coming of Christ but find ourselves speechless when he states, 'I don't know what you have done but there seems to be peace in your hamlet at last. The neighbours are speaking to each other. No more complaints.'

Leaning back on his chair, he blows his smoke in a spiral towards the ceiling, inhales again and lets out a satisfied sigh. 'It's heaven.'

What have we done, I wonder. We've been cordial, tried to listen, to hear everyone's perspective and learn the customs of the place. Only when Peter picked up a book on what is acceptable practice do we realise how many mistakes we have made along the way. Don't ask the French their names and don't use them. Don't call on them. Wait to be introduced. Always sit them around the table. Never discuss money.

We seem to have broken all the major taboos yet, despite the gaffes, they are beginning to accept us. We have regularly prayed a Lord's Prayer, 'your kingdom come', over the place because where the king reigns, there will be peace between neighbours. And we have confirmation that it has indeed begun, when the last thing Henri tells us before we leave is that he and Roland have started chatting to each other in a very civilised manner. Who knows whether it will continue when we are no longer there, when they battle over the boundaries without Peter's offices as an intermediary but we think it might.

More than anything I have learnt to measure achievement very differently – not in professional status or salary but in living as we are meant to live, participating as fully as we can in the lives around us. Perhaps listening to our neighbours, sharing in their joys and their pain, digging trenches, planting trees, sharing what God has given to us with those around us, walking through the minefield that is our village with all the integrity we can muster, is the alternative version of productivity. After all, in the fullness of time people will only remember what we were, not what we did or said. Perhaps it's the most important lesson of our sabbatical, the best preparation for the passage of the years.

And what of our beloved land? The garden will go to seed or sprout wild flowers. There will be flood or drought and the stream will either fill or dry out. Some new trees will blossom, others will perish. Planting trees is much like prayer. We may not actually live to see results of our efforts – but it's a great investment for the future. We have no idea what we will find in June, for the land will re-establish its mastery until we can give it permanent care.

Could we cope with rural life? If it's not the coypu that need dealing with, it's the little mole that has started tunnelling under and turning over the front lawn. I'm still too townie to know the mole's breeding habits – and whether we'll have any lawn left. If it's not flies, it's slugs, or mice with diarrhoea who manage to get into the cellar. Or Lavale's sheep manoeuvring their way through a hole in the fence smaller than they are, so that they can eat our tender saplings. Or toads diving into the swimming pool. We can't even go into the boggy under-growth without wellies for fear of vipers. But we are slowly learning to live in harmony with the animal kingdom – wild boar roaming freely across our land, lizards trying to climb through bedroom windows, wag-tails nesting in the gutters, woodpeckers chipping holes in the shutters. In the early summer we can expect to see golden orioles, hoopoes and kingfishers, a magnificent variety of unusual birds, as well as the herons who have adopted us. I've never been a twitcher before. Abby says it must come with age.

There is no doubt who is boss, of course. A coypu swam happily across the pond before we left today – with five babies in tow. *Salut Madame*, you win.

'Next winter we must . . .' Peter says, then checks him-self. We shall not be here next winter – nor possibly for the next eight. When Peter had his last sabbatical, some thirteen years ago, he went home a youngish man, with a fairly clear vision for his future ministry. At 45 you still dream dreams, make long-term plans. At 57 you just hope you'll still be here tomorrow, that you'll actually live to see the retirement you plan for. Nothing is guar-anteed.

We have spent the past months surrounded by con-temporaries in the process of retiring, many of them much earlier than we can. It has unsettled us, pre-empt-ing what is not yet, swinging us between the losses and gains of ageing. We want to stay. We don't want to stay. We must live for now and thank God for what is. We are not, for the moment, retiring. We are – *avec une petite regrette* – ready to go back to another however many years of full-time ministry, to potentially and hopefully our best years yet. The adventure will continue – there and here – with or without a stipend. The emotional see-saw certainly isn't comfortable but it has been necessary.

Our first granddaughter is due in March. I'm already imagining her here in a dinghy on the lake, making dams across Peter's trench, building a tree house, cycling up and down the paths he has swathed out. I'm going to speak French to her, that's for sure. If this is to feel like home, she must speak the language. And even if I never live to see it, we have been given the chance to pave the way for that in these three wonderful gift months.

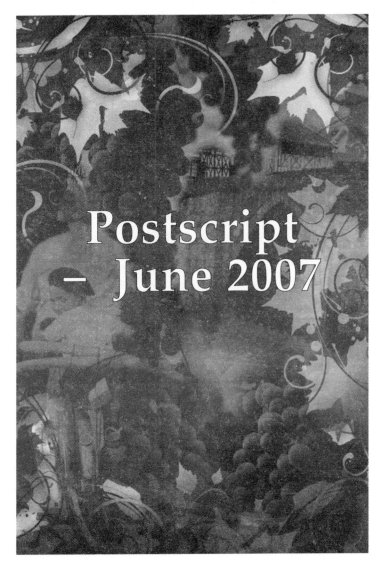

Postscript
– June 2007

Monsieur Gehl, the *géomètre*, finally arrives in his bat-
tered old jeep to place the boundary markers.

'Can I offer you a drink?' I ask him as he drags his
wellingtons out of the boot.

He wags a finger at me.

'Ah, non, Madame, we are camels. We have learnt not
to drink. If I take as much as a cup of water from you it
could be construed as a bribe.'

As he changes into his statutory footwear, Peter asks
him whether he knows that there were laws concerning
the boundaries between neighbours from the beginning
of Jewish civilisation. He shows him a verse in
Deuteronomy that says, 'You shall not move neighbour's boundary marker.'

'*Tiens*,' says Monsieur Gehl, shaking his head, clearly
impressed. 'My job is over three thousand years old.
Now that really is something.'

He all but slaps Peter on the back and sets off
whistling.

Not for long. The situation soon becomes acrimo-
nious. I had gone back home to sit on the verandah and
read a book in peace and quiet but the noise from the
other side of the field is making concentration impossible. The commotion is so loud I can hardly believe my
ears. Can one man make such a racket? It certainly
seems he can, since Peter is standing calmly by the
géomètre with a rather bemused expression on his face. I
head out for a ringside view.

Monsieur Lavale is not a happy man and that's an
understatement. In fact, he is devastated with the *géomètre's* assessment of where the boundary should be –

two metres further into his own land than he anticipated. In a paroxysm of rage, grief and blood pressure, he has turned worryingly red and is leaping up and down, shouting rudely, 'This bit of land is mine, it's mine, it's mine, my grandfather said so. And my grandfather was right.'

'Monsieur Lavale,' commands the *géomètre*, putting a stop to his work until he has the farmer's full attention, 'if you do not control yourself immediately, I will report your behaviour to the court and ask them to prosecute you for your rudeness to one of its officers. Monsieur Lambert,' he urges the solicitor's assistant, 'take charge of your client, or he could find himself in deep trouble.'

As the solicitor grabs Lavale's elbow and yanks him several steps back, the *géomètre* turns to Peter and says with a wink, 'Monsieur Guinness, please use that excellent mower of yours to remove some of the undergrowth so that I can prove to Monsieur Lavale beyond all measure of doubt where the boundary line should be.'

The mower is so noisy that it drowns Lavale's wailing, a fact that has not been lost on Monsieur Gehl, who heaves a sigh of relief and continues his painstaking work, alternately checking the Napoleonic map and measuring the distance between trees. It seems to be an art rather than a science and in the end, to pacify our neighbour, he concedes and gives him three of our oaks. We are magnanimous. We can afford to be. Our boundary is intact. He won't dare cut the trees down – that we now know for certain. What is more, it has become manifestly obvious that if it were Henri who cut down some of the hedgerows, and we now doubt it, knowing his greater love of the environment, then it was his own that he removed and neither Henri nor we can therefore be sued. The Napoleonic map, like the Bible, is sacrosanct.

We send Monsieur Gehl off with the promise of delivering some bottles of his beloved Guinness.

He smiles with evident pleasure and taps the side of his nose. 'Once the court case is over.'

'But of course,' we concede.

In fact, in the coming months, all the claims against Henri collapse and one of his accusers has had to pay him compensation for their malicious allegations. Was Janice's account of him as a bully true? We now have reason to doubt her interpretation of that particular encounter. It is always worth listening to two sides of every story. We don't doubt that Henri can be as volatile as a bull if provoked. But we have no intention of finding out. In our experience, he has never been anything other than courteous and considerate and we take as we find. And like him more and more.

And the strange nightmares that haunted our sleeping hours during those few months? Possibly our spiritual antennae were picking up the disturbance in the local atmosphere. Murderous thoughts and malice can have a tangible impact on the environment.

Alternatively, unknown to us, we might have been sensing a certain unrest at home, for we went back, as so many do after a period of extended leave, to discover a melting pot of tensions in one or two key relationships and the inevitable heartache they cause. The crisis is past. Resolution has released the energy and vision Peter couldn't somehow access during our sabbatical itself. Now there is peaceful sleep, quiet days and an overwhelming sense of gratitude for all we have been given. And the promise of the prophet Isaiah that was given like a blown kiss from God on the day of the Tribunal, hovers around our hearts and holds them in its wonder.

'My people will live in peaceful dwelling places, in secure homes, in undisturbed places of rest.'

Postscript

When I talked about a volatile economy and fragile stock market so many months ago I had no idea how frighteningly imminent that was. My private pension has evaporated. Peter's is worth a third of its value in France, as the pound tumbles against the euro. Despite my predictions, we feel rather winded.

An even greater shock has been the sudden death of our friendly mayor from a stroke, while only in his sixties. At our last encounter he introduced me to a local council member as 'the priest's wife.'

'They have it right in the Church of England. They marry,' he said, with a knowing grin.

Will the next mayor be as sympathetic?

His death was followed within weeks by the suicide of the postmistress. I keep thinking of her curt manner and down-turned mouth and wonder, had I known how unhappy she was, whether I would have done or said anything different, as I cashed my cheques and bought my stamps. But what?

The village is in mourning. I wish we could be with them.

Patrick and Marinette have just spent a week with us. There was an intake of breath as they shared the story of their church with ours. They described the dearth of spiritual life in France, the anxiety of bringing up four children without a church youth club or safe peer group, the strain of scrabbling around for a single musician to lead worship every week, and the unanticipated sorrow that many of the English ex-pats were now leaving for home, unable to afford the cost of living. Few church-going, English holiday-makers have any idea of the story behind the cheeses, the wine, and the croissants.

Their visit helped restore our flagging resolve. Madness as it may seem, we still have that irrational certainty that our lives are inseparably bound up with the French. Several ministers – French and English – broken by the strain of the job, have contacted us in the last few months, desperate for somewhere to rest, talk and recuperate. We could perhaps provide a little of that. In the current circumstances, it would involve much more of a faith venture than we bargained for. But that may not be a bad thing for worried sparrows like me, who struggle to commit themselves to the heavenly investment company.

I haven't bought nearly as many clothes since I came back. I shan't need them. I shall grow fruit and vegetables, make pies and tarts, jams and chutneys, and become an eccentric rural dame in dangly earrings and baggy pullovers. And since man cannot live by rhubarb alone, we shall have to trust for the rest of the food on our table. The Christian's last resort will become our first – as it should be.

So all that's left is to resolve the when. I hope it isn't long.

**For more information or resources please go to
www.micheleguinness.co.uk**

Glossary

l'aimable	literally 'in a friendly way', legal phrase for informal resolving of boundary disputes
acte de vente	official papers for a house sale
agriculteur	agriculturalist, land-owning farmer
alors	well then
assistante	school assistant
Au clair de la lune	By the light of the moon – French folk song
aujourd'ui	today
au revoir	goodbye
bavarois	a kind of cake
bien	fine
bien sûr	of course
bon	good
bon courage	good courage – ie good luck
bonjour	hello – literally, good day
bornage	boundary
bouche	mouth
bouchon	traffic jam
boulangerie	bakery
bricolage	DIY
brocantes	secondhand furniture shops
brocanteur	seller of secondhand furniture or antiques
canard	duck
caractère	a character
cêpe	a kind of mushroom
charcuterie	a shop that sells cold cooked meats, patés etc

château	castle, large house
chéri	darling
chocolatier	a professional chocolate-maker
choux	cabbage
confit	a conserve
concubin	concubine
conjoint	spouse
croyant	believer
curé	priest (Roman Catholic)
de	of, from
demande d'avis de reception	request for an acknowledgement of receipt
desolé	sorry
eau de javel	bleach
eau de vive	pure liqueur
l'étang	pond
évangéliste	evangelist
évangelique	evangelical
farcie	stuffing
fauteuil roulant	wheelchair
fermier	farmer
foire	a market
frère	brother
froideur	coldness
gêle	ice
Gentille Alouette	gentle dove - French folk song
géomètre	boundary surveyor
gigot	chop
gîte	rented property
glisser	to slip
hein	huh?
in situ	in place
interdit	forbidden
jambon	ham

j'adore ça	I love that
je suis	I am
je te plumerai la tête	I stroke your head
joli	pretty
joyeuse fête	Happy holiday
lac	lake
lapin	rabbit
le maire	the mayor
lieu noir	coley (lit. black place)
longère	traditional French farmhouses
mairie	the town hall
maison	house
maître	master
milles feuilles	cake made of puff pastry and vanilla custard
nettoyer	to clean
nez	nose
non	no
notaire	solicitor or lawyer
nous sommes	we are
office du tourisme	tourist office
oui	yes
pain d'épice	spice bread
papier	paper
pasteur	pastor
patiner	to skate
patissier	pastry chef
peint	paint
personnel en grève	staff on strike
Pineau	a liqueur from the Charente region
plus grand	bigger
pompiers	firemen
poule	chicken

près	near
presbytère	minister's house
proprietaire	owner
que c'est joli	that's pretty
qu'est-ce que tu fais?	What are you doing?
rillettes	rough kind of paté
rôti de boeuf	roast beef
salut	hi
tarte au citron	lemon tart
tarte aux pommes	apple tart
tarte tatin	a kind of upsidedown, caramelised apple tart
tartiner	to spread
tête	head
tiens	really?
trou perdu	literally 'lost hole', back of beyond
tutoie	to address someone as 'tu', not 'vous' the formal way of saying you
truffes	truffles
venez	come
la vie française	the French life
vos	your
zut	Blow! (or similar exclamation)